DEDICATION

To my dad and grandpa John, for taking the time to teach a little kid to fish.

CONTENTS

Preface

*"The charm of fishing is that it is the pursuit of what is elusive
but attainable, a perpetual series of occasions for hope."*
— John Buchan

Just before sunrise, on a warm morning in mid-June in southern Wisconsin, I was preparing to launch my boat, and I could hardly hide my sense of excitement. I had been out fishing several times already that year, but this was the first time I was out by myself. I love companions while fishing, but there is something particularly magical about fishing when you have nothing but your own thoughts and nature to act as a muse. As I headed out on the lake there was light but balmy west wind which scarcely created even a ripple on the water. I knew the pristine conditions would only last a few hours as soon enough the lake would fill with a myriad of folks participating in their favorite water sport. For now, at least, the water was mine.

The lake was normal enough, at several miles long with possibly a mile of width in a spot or two. It had been mostly settled, with about ninety percent or more of the shoreline dotted with houses. It was a fertile body of water, with a great deal of cover both man-made and otherwise. The lake was best known for bass, however, it also contained panfish, walleye, musky and my target for the day; big northern pike. My normal style of fishing revolves around artificial lures, but today I was targeting trophy pike with live bait. My minnow bucket was full of 8"-12" suckers, the large sort that I hoped would be irresistible to the giant northern I knew prowled the depths of the lake.

As I neared my spot, I slowed the boat well in advance so as to slide in with as little disturbance to the pristine water as possible. When the boat came to a stop, I dropped the trolling motor into the water and flipped on my fish finder to find the ideal location. As I nudged the boat north looking for that perfect depth of water, I was completely floored by the beauty of the rising sun. As it peaked over the trees on the eastern bank the sky turned a radiant hue of red. I sat for a few moments soaking up the warm rays of the newly arrived day and reflected on the beauty that is so easy to take for granted in the daily hustle of life. Just then near the shore, I heard an all too familiar smack and splash that indicated a surface hit by a hungry fish only yards away. With that, I was back to my task of landing a trophy pike. For this particular trip, I had two rods set up with a slip bobber. On one, I had 12lb line and a leader combined with a slightly smaller hook that I planned to use with the smaller suckers. On the other rod, I had heavy braided line with a strong 2/0 hook for use with the largest suckers. First I tossed out my smaller rig in hopes of landing a couple quick fish. As any good fisherman knows, a good fish story cannot be told without first catching a fish. As my bobber splashed the water I set the pole down with the intent of baiting up my other rod. I had scarcely picked the second rod up when my fisherman's sixth sense kicked in and I glanced back at my line just in time to see my bobber slipping under the surface. It had been in place only seconds and I already had a bite! I grabbed the rod and yanked it back hammering home a hard hook set. Immediately I could feel that telltale tug and rapid undulations on the other end of the line. Out of second nature I muttered, "fish on!" and the fight commenced. A short time later I brought the fish near the surface and was able to see that it was indeed a beautiful midsized northern. I had hooked it right in the side of the mouth. As I brought it to the boat, I leaned over and extracted the hook while avoiding the mouthful of teeth for the fish so aptly named the "water wolf." The action continued like this for the better part of a half-hour. I hooked fish after fish only seconds after the bobber had settled. At this stage, while I had not boated any exceptional fish, I had already enjoyed one of

7

the best mornings of pike fishing I had experienced in years. The sun still hung low in the sky, and my arms were tired from reeling in fish. Life just doesn't get much better than this. As time progressed the action began to slow, and I was finally able to consider getting my larger rod in the water with some bait that might attract a true monster.

I reached in the minnow bucket and picked out the biggest bait I could grab hold of. As I cast the bait out I could already envision the battle that was about to ensue. First seconds and then minutes passed without any action. My bobber kept me guessing as the large sucker on the other end lazily swam about beneath it. After a few more minutes I was just getting ready to check to make sure nothing had gone awry with the setup when my bobber suddenly jerked to the side and then violently plowed under the water and disappeared from sight. I knew instantly this was a big fish, and I also knew that I had to resist the urge to set the hook immediately. Fish of this caliber often grab a large bait fish and simply hold it in their mouth waiting for it to stop struggling before they devour it. I needed to give it just a little time before driving home a hook set. One-one-thousand, two-one-thousand, three-one-thousand. It seemed like an eternity. I picked up the rod and gave it a powerful jerk to set the hook. As any fisherman can attest, there is always something unusual about a hook set on a real trophy. I could tell instantly I had hooked a bigger fish. It took several more seconds for the real battle to ensue. The fish peeled out drag and doubled over the rod. The battle went on for several minutes before I was finally able to begin bringing the fish to the surface. As I played the fish ever closer to the boat, I tried to balance my rod in one hand, while reaching for the net with the other. It was during this process that I got the first glimpse of the fish. My lunker was indeed a trophy, but it was no pike. For northern waters, it was a behemoth largemouth bass teetering close to the 8lb mark. With the battle winding down, I was able to land the fish and get it aboard with little difficulty. So there I sat, in the early morning sun, holding my biggest Wisconsin bass, basking in one of my more memorable fishing experiences. That trip embodies so much of what is magical about fishing; communing with Mother Nature, the sport of a great battle, and the uncertainty of just what is lurking beneath the surface.

I opened with this story because it's about something we've all experienced; wonder on the water when the fish are practically jumping in the boat. What though, makes those days so different from a day when the fish simply won't cooperate? Fishing is filled with old adages that attempt to offer explanations, "When the wind is from the west the fishing is best, when the wind is from the east the fishing is least." "When the cows are lying down, the fish won't bite." "Red in the morning a sailors warning, red at night a sailors delight." We will see in this book, some of these sayings have grains of truth at their foundation, while others are virtually baseless. As fishermen, we must be careful of a great danger that haunts much of the fishing world: Illusory correlation. Illusory correlations result from our natural propensity to recall events better than non-events. For instance, many anglers use peak period calendars that can be found in many popular fishing magazines. When a bite happens to align with one of these forecasted peaks, anglers tend to remember this "event" and file it away in their minds as a supportive data point. Conversely, when fishing is poor during a forecasted period our natural tendency is to forget the non-event or attribute the poor fishing to some other factor such as the weather. Fishing with its many complex and ever changing variables is particularly susceptible to the trap of illusory correlation. I know I'm not the only one who's been skunked on a day when the wind was blowing beautifully from the west.

This is the reason that data is so incredibly powerful when it comes to determining which causal factors truly have an impact on fishing. Whether we are talking catch rates or economic trends. Data matters. It separates fact from fiction. It relieves us of age-old bias and it positions us, perhaps for the first time, to truly understand our sport. This book is my humble attempt to share some of the ideas and insights I've been able to gather from years worth of studying the data.

Key Concept:

The High Percentage Fisherman: High Percentage Fishermen pick the lake, the day, and the time they are going to fish based on information. They love just being on the water, but they also love catching fish. Their time is at a premium so they bet their chips on data-based strategies that are likely to yield the biggest payoff.

Book Structure

Section 1: Big Bass Basics
This section covers the fundamentals of big bass behavior and summarizes the findings of some of the world's greatest big bass fishermen. It also examines the basic biology of largemouth bass and the impact of various forms of pressure.

Section 2: The Data
This section covers the statistical findings extracted from a database of more than 40,000 freshwater predator fish catches.

Section 1

Big Bass Basics

On the Shoulders of Giants

"Our tradition is that of the first man who sneaked away to the creek when the tribe did not really need fish."
– Roderick Haig-Brown

While he was not the first person to utter the phrase, Sir Isaac Newton famously said, "If I have seen farther than others it is because I have stood on the shoulders of giants." I think this quote is a fitting title for this chapter as it will examine the key findings of some of the best big bass fishermen the world has ever known. Before we use statistics to help light our path forward, it is important to know how far we have come and where we stand today in terms of concepts and fundamental principles.

In the storied halls of big bass fishing, there are three names, Doug Hannon, John Hope, and Bill Murphy that stand out amongst the crowd for being pioneers in the field of fishing for giants. Between the three of them, they have an unparalleled resume of over a thousand fish weighing more than 10lbs. For decades, each of these men studied big bass, observed them in their environment and developed exhaustive theories about their behavior. Each ultimately wrote a book that when taken together constitute a veritable bible of big bass fishing. (*Doug Hannon, Big Bass Magic 1986. John Hope, Trackin' Trophies 1996, and Bill Murphy, In Pursuit of Giant Bass 1992*) However, there has been one quiet but consistent criticism of these works by many anglers. On the surface, they seem to draw different conclusions, particularly about where big bass are most likely to be found. In this chapter, we will explore the key findings of each author. I'll argue that there is a common thread amongst each of these big bass anglers that may lead to a unified theory that can help High Percentage Fishermen increase their odds of catching the fish of a lifetime.

Doug Hannon, "Big Bass Magic"

Doug Hannon, originally a native of Canada moved to the US as a child. While attending college at Tulane University in New Orleans, he met his future wife Lynn Peters, a Texas native. Lynn introduced Hannon to bass fishing and he was soon addicted to the sport. In 1970, Hannon and his wife Lynn relocated to central Florida where Hannon began a decades' long study of big bass behavior. Hannon primarily fished smaller remote natural lakes and rivers and over the course of his fishing career he racked up an astounding 800+ fish that weighed in at over 10lbs. Later becoming known as the "Bass Professor," Hannon frequently used scuba gear to observe bass and maintained a large holding tank in his back yard for observing big bass behavior across all seasons. Hannon combined years' worth of on the water observation with detailed knowledge of bass biology to establish compelling insight into big bass behavior. Hannon believed the biggest bass in Florida were most likely to come from latitudes between Tampa and Gainesville. He believed these fish were far enough south to have an extended growing season, but also far enough north to avoid the shortened life spans common in the warmest southern waters as a result of metabolic burnout. He caught most of his giant fish on live bait in the middle of the day and he believed the biggest fish preferred shallow water claiming as many as 90% of his fish came from 3 feet of water or less. He had a strong preference for fishing thick grassy weed beds in close proximity to natural springs which he believed moderated temperatures which helped create ideal conditions for big bass to grow. He advocated fishing remote waters or areas of the lake that other fishermen wouldn't fish because of accessibility. He freely admitted that finding such locations was becoming increasingly difficult because of increases in fishing pressure.

He believed artificial lures were best in low light conditions and at night. He also advocated the use of silent lures and stealthy approaches. As outlined in his many writings, some of Hannon's key findings are as follows:

-High water temperatures can shorten the life span of big bass through dramatically increased metabolic rates making giants a near biological impossibility in the warmest southern waters.

-Target areas with low fishing pressure. Areas may have low pressure either because they are geographically remote, or because they have structure or cover that makes them difficult to reach by less motivated anglers.

-90% of big bass come from less than 3 feet of water.

-As fishing pressure increases, big bass may be forced to move to deeper water.

-Big bass are highly territorial and have small home ranges.

-Visual and auditory stealth are extremely important when pursuing big bass. Hannon would even go so far as to camouflage the bottom of his boat.

-Live bait, shiners in particular, are the best big bass bait.

-Plastic worms are the dominate artificial big bass bait.

-Artificial lures typically only out produce live bait in low light conditions.

-Big bass feed aggressively during the middle of the day.

-The spawn or low light conditions generally create the best odds for average fishermen to catch big fish.

-There is a major connection between natural springs and the presence of big bass. While often low in oxygen content, springs moderate temperatures.

-Bass are influenced by moon phases.

-Big bass tend to stay in a depth range that typically did not vary by more than 8 feet.

-The convergence of multiple forms of structure and cover created ideal big bass habitat.

John Hope, "Trackin' Trophies"

In the late 1980's John Hope was a fishing guide at Houston County Lake, a 1,500-acre lake in East Texas. As an accomplished big bass angler, much like Doug Hannon, Hope became increasingly interested in the behaviors of big bass. After learning about electronic tracking methods used to track other animals, Hope got the idea to attempt tracking big bass. Initially, it began half out of curiosity and half as a marketing ploy to drum up business for his guide service. Over the better part of a decade, Hope completed a variety of tracking studies predominantly in Texas that focused on the movement and habits of trophy-sized bass. Over the years, dozens of fish were tracked ranging in size from a few pounds to true lunkers north of 15lbs. The bodies of water Hope tracked fish in ranged from a few hundred acres all the way up to the behemoth Sam Rayburn Reservoir at 114,000 acres. Hope completed the study with astounding persistence. At some points staying on the water for days at a time through rain or shine, sleeping in his boat to ensure all movements of the fish were captured. He stayed with the studies through all seasons in water temperatures ranging from the low 40s to well into the 90s.

In 1986, one of the first bass Hope studied closely was a 10lber on Houston County Lake nicknamed "Wanda," after his wife. (A full two years before the hit comedy that shared the name.) Hope tracked the fish for over a year, catching her multiple times before she was ultimately caught and mounted by another angler. One of the key findings of the study was that the fish had a small home range, rarely straying more than a few hundred yards to feed. Hope completed similar studies dozens of times with large fish from all over the state and was ultimately able to establish some principals that forever changed his approach to chasing trophy fish.

-Big fish have preferred depth ranges. Ranges were labeled as shallow (0-8 feet), mid-layer (8-12 feet), and deep layer (12+ feet). No fish in the study had a feeding range that varied by more than 10 feet. Mid-range and deep water fish only ventured to shallower waters when biology dictated they do so during the spawn.

-Big fish have small ranges. Once a fish reaches 7lbs or so, it establishes a home range and a preferred depth, outside of the spawn big fish rarely leave their preferred range and depth layer. Hope stated big fish had ranges that were typically located close to their spawning flats and rarely exceeded more than a few hundred yards in size.

-Big fish were highly predictable in that they precisely followed a daily routine.

-Big fish tended to be in either a negative or positive feeding mood. When in a negative mood, the fish were usually suspended, and virtually impossible to coax into biting. Conversely, when in a positive mood, the fish roamed their home range, typically along a break line, near the shallower end of their preferred depth layer looking for a meal.

-Feeding cycles generally lasted 2 hours, punctuated by long periods of inactivity while suspended.

-Feeding cycles began about a half-hour before dusk and ended a half hour after dawn.

-All large bass Hope studied, fed periodically during the day but they were predominately nocturnal feeders.

-Weather systems seemed to have little or no impact on larger fish, although it did sometimes influence bait fish, which then indirectly influenced habits of the bass.

-The only weather related phenomena Hope noted that significantly impacted fishing were rapid or dramatic changes in water levels.

-Large fish are difficult to catch, not because they reside in ultra-secretive hard to reach spots, but because they are suspended and are inactive for large portions of the day when most anglers are fishing.

-Hope said, "Fishing pressure eliminates trophy bass in shallow water. Anglers do not allow very many of them to get to be trophy size. In my opinion, if a fish lives in shallow water and manages to reach six or seven pounds, the fishing pressure and boating pressure alone make it move out and become a mid-layer bass."

Funnel points

Another key concept discovered by Hope was the importance of funnel points. Hope believed that one of the best approaches to catching big bass was to target them at so-called funnel points during high probability feeding times. For reasons we shall see, indirectly this is a High Percentage Fishing method. Hope noted that most bass anglers tended to fish shallow water. He also knew that fishing deep water effectively was difficult. He, therefore, hypothesized that targeting bass in the mid-range depths would present the best overall chance of landing trophy class fish. As part of his studies, Hope had been marking the location of his biggest catches on topographical maps for years. Eventually, an observation jumped out at him; most of his biggest catches were coming off structure that shared a common trait. They were funnel points, that is to say, "areas of the lake where troughs, ditches, or draws natural to the contour of the lake created what amounted to an underwater highway." Particularly attractive funnels narrowed to pinch points only a few yards wide ending in cover such as grass or timber. Hope hypothesized funnel points corralled big fish into tight areas as they moved around the lake from offshore resting spots to shallow water hunting grounds. Over the years, Hope refined this approach to focus on fishing these funnel points during high percentage times around dawn and dusk, noting that if an angler did this consistently, it would not take him long to land a trophy. The figure on the next page shows an example of a typical funnel.

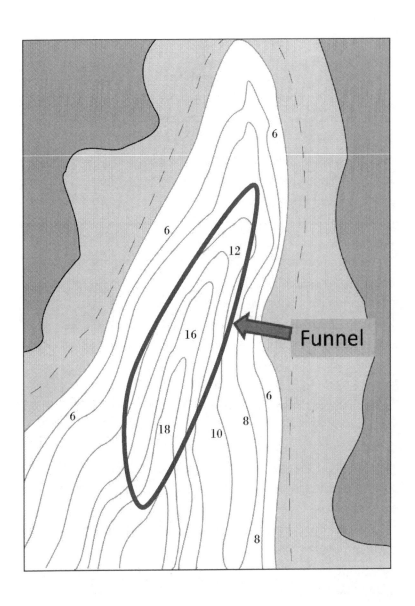

Bill Murphy – "In Pursuit of Giants"

Before Hannon, before Hope, and for decades beginning in the 1960s Bill Murphy was considered by many to be the finest big bass angler in the country. Hailing from the San Diego area, his reputation in Southern California was nothing short of legendary. His resume is impressive to say the least, hundreds of bass over 10lbs, nearly 40 fish over 13lbs, and a handful over 15lbs including his personal best a 17lbs 1 oz leviathan finessed from the depths of St. Vincent Reservoir. A pioneer of deep water structure fishing before the time of depth finders, Murphy compiled over 30 years of big bass fishing experience into his masterpiece on the subject *"In Pursuit of Giants."* Murphy was a pioneer who shirked many popular conventions and fished the way the fish told him to fish. Often his techniques focused on finesse fishing live bait or soft plastic in deep water haunts favored by big bass in some of the most highly pressured lakes in the country. Some of his key findings on big bass behavior include the following:

-Big bass patterns are completely different from small bass patterns. Small bass tend to be shallow where smaller prey is readily available. Large bass prefer the safety of deep water and the availability of larger prey.

-Big bass are highly territorial and have small home ranges.

-Big bass move progressively deeper as fishing pressure increases.

-Big bass are never more than a few tail strokes away from deep water.

-Big bass favor outer edges close to deep water, particularly multi-direction drop offs near multiple kinds of structure/cover.

-Big bass are largely unaffected by weather changes, in terms of feeding habits, position, and depth.

-Three of the most effective big bass techniques are live bait, trolling, and anchoring.

-Stealth is a key component to catching big bass.

-Emphasized the importance of the spot over the lure or the presentation; you can't catch bass that are not there.

-He believed plastic worms were the dominate artificial lure for big bass.

-He believed shiners were likely the best overall bait for big bass.

-He favored black baits.

-He favored mastering a few home lakes.

-He believed the spawning period was the best chance for average anglers to catch big bass.

Multi-directional Drop-offs

One type of structure particularly favored by Murphy was hard bottomed multi-directional drop offs. (Example on the next page.) These structures are easily identifiable on topographical maps. They allow bass to remain in a small home range, offer flexibility in optimal ambush positions based on wind and current, and provide ready access to deep water. Additionally, these structures typically cover large vertical distances, allowing bass to remain in their home range during frequent water fluctuations common in deep water west coast

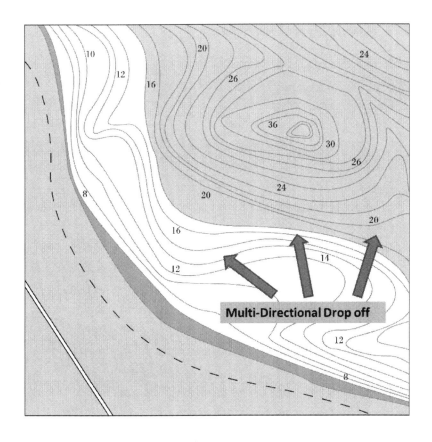

Multi-Directional Drop off

reservoirs. Murphy believed the best multi-directional drop offs were generally near the deepest water in the area and had hard bottoms devoid of decaying vegetation with sparse or intermittent cover.

HP Tip: Depth finders can help determine bottom composition. With factory settings on newer Lowrance and Hummingbird models, hard bottoms will generally show up on color fish finders as a thick yellow band. Softer, muddier bottoms will typically show up as darker red or blue.

Comparing Big Bass Ideas

On the surface, it seems as though Hope, Hannon, and Murphy disagree on a great many aspects of big bass behavior. Hannon claims 90% of all his big bass were caught in 3 feet or less. Hope claims the best thing an angler can do to increase his odds of catching a trophy is to fish the 8-12 foot mid-layer. Finally, Murphy states that the common factor amongst all his big fish was deep water. While seemingly contradictory, I believe these observed differences concerning the location of large bass is principally driven by regional differences in the fishing pressure that each angler encountered. There is an ancient proverb about a group of blind men who each feel different parts of an elephant and then try to come to an agreement about the nature of the creature. The first man felt the trunk and said the creature was like a snake. The second felt the legs and said it was like a group of mighty pillars. The third felt the ears and said it was like two large burlap blankets. Agreement amongst the group seemed impossible. Each man was correct in his perception of the particular part of the elephant, but only when each man began to consider the whole animal in the context of the others perspective were they able to truly get a picture of what an elephant actually looks like. In much the same way, Hannon, Hope, and Murphy, all accurately described big bass behavior in their particular region of the country, but only when we consider each of these descriptions in the context of their local conditions do we finally get a broader sense of true big bass behavior. I believe the common thread that links the observed behavior of trophy fish in all three locations is fishing pressure.

Hannon's beliefs are largely based on conditions that no longer exist in much of the country. He formulated many of his theories in the warm shallow waters of central Florida in the 1970's when Walt Disney World wasn't even a household name. Fishing pressure was a fraction of the levels encountered in today's angling reality. In warm pristine conditions bass no doubt favor the shallow depths and approaches Hannon advocated. However, in today's world of increased fishing pressure, many big bass have either moved progressively deeper in our lakes or as John Hope suggested, fishing selection pressure has simply removed big bass in the shallow portions of lakes. That is to say, **the average depth of trophy class fish is largely a function of fishing pressure**. In Hope's world fishing moderately pressured lakes in Texas, this meant big bass were likely to be found in the mid-layer of lakes in the 8-12 foot range. *Murphy, on the other hand, was fishing the highly pressured lakes of California and so trophy bass were primarily found on deep lake structure. The notion that fishing pressure influences bass location is an example of the theory of efficient markets. In economics, the theory goes that investment markets are so efficient that it is very rare to find an undervalued asset. The argument states that it is more likely that you have incorrectly assigned a value to the asset than that the asset is truly undervalued. After all, if an asset were undervalued, the market would have noticed and corrected the price. The corollary to fishing is that most fishermen are good at fishing shallow water, thus, there are not many big fish left in shallow water. If they were there they would have already been caught and "released into grease" or stunted from repeat trauma while being caught.

*Some have suggested big bass in California are deep because they frequently gorge on trout which have been stocked and typically reside in deeper portions of the lake. There may be some truth to this notion, but it does not explain many large fish, some in excess of 20lbs that have been plumbed from the depths of California's many lakes not stocked with trout.

Sure, you may come across the occasional lunker shallow, but in general, finding them there is a low probability strategy. To add a little color to this concept, consider two economists who were out fishing Lake Fork during the spawn. While cruising the shoreline, they came across a huge female on a bed that looked to be at least 13 pounds! Both being familiar with the efficient market theory simply couldn't believe what they were seeing. They decided to pull off the bed and head to deeper water to discuss the matter. They engaged in a lengthy and spirited debate. One argued that it must be their lucky day and they've stumbled across a true giant. The other argued that they must be vastly overestimating the size of the fish because any fish that size and that shallow would have already been caught by other fishermen. Finally, they agreed to head back to the bed to confirm once and for all who was right. When they looked back to shore, they saw another boat sitting just off the bed, reeling in a monster 13-pound fish. The moral of the story is that big fish don't last long shallow! It is for this reason, the greater the fishing pressure, the deeper you should fish if you are targeting trophies. If you are fishing for numbers you may be better off shallow, particularly in spring as shallow waters are the warmest; the fish in those waters have higher metabolic rates requiring them to feed more frequently. Several smaller fish that Hope documented in his studies never ventured into water deeper than 6 feet. Hope also noted that smaller fish feed more frequently, up to as much as 20 hours a day as compared to 12 hours a day for fish over 7lbs.

Outside of regional differences that we have reconciled with fishing pressure, Hope, Hannon, and Murphy have remarkable agreement on many other big bass behaviors. The graph on the next page and the section that follows summarizes many of their key points of agreement.

Concept	Doug Hannon	John Hope	Bill Murphy
Shallow pressured water is a poor producer of trophy fish		✓	✓
Weather has little impact on trophy fish	✓	✓	✓
Big bass have dormant periods	✓		✓
Most trophy fish come from deep water	✓	✓	✓
Most trophy fish come from shallow water	✓		
Most trophy fish come from medium depths		✓	✓
Live bait is a dominate trophy bass tactic			✓
Stealth is extremely important to catch trophy bass	✓	✓	✓
Spots are more important that baits	✓	✓	✓
Trophy bass have a small home range	✓	✓	✓
Fish low pressure areas/depths	✓	✓	✓
The heavier the fishing pressure the deeper big bass are	✓	✓	✓
Plastic worms are the best artificial bass bait	✓	✓	✓
Night fishing yields more trophies than daylight / hour	✓	✓	✓
Spring is the best time to catch a trophy (for most anglers)	✓	✓	✓
Emphasis on low light levels	✓	✓	✓
Big bass have preferred depth layers	✓	✓	✓
Small bass patterns differ dramatically from big bass	✓	✓	✓
Anchoring is an important technique			✓

Live Bait, Trolling, and Anchoring

I once spoke with a fisheries biologist and a big bass expert in South East Texas and asked him if he had any advice on the best approach to finding and landing a trophy fish in the shortest amount of time. His advice was simple: "One thing you can do, especially in public waters, is to pot-lick (use live bait). You'll be accused of being everything other than a child of God, but it is the best way to increase your odds dramatically." All three of our big bass guru's would agree with the importance of using live bait. Hope and Murphy, in particular, were big fans of Shiners. In many circles, it is viewed as somehow less sporting, and certainly if we are talking degrees of difficulty catching a trophy on artificial lures is generally more difficult. This book, however, is about High Percentage Fishing, and live bait techniques are legal, challenging in their own right and one surefire method to improve your chances of success. The reality is most big fish have seen a huge number of artificial lures throughout their life. Tricking the wise old beasts into biting real prey food is much easier than using artificial lures. The primary limitation of live bait is that the technique does not lend itself well to covering large amounts of water. To be effective, anglers need to have specific knowledge of areas that hold trophy fish.

Trolling is another method looked down upon by some bass fishermen. If you want to cast, by all means cast. If you want to catch fish, trolling should be an arrow in your quiver. One of the huge advantages of trolling is that it allows you to cover large amounts of water quickly and is one of the few techniques that can keep baits in deep water strike zones for extended periods of time. When trolling deep crankbaits, you may be putting baits in front of fish that have never seen lures.

Consider for a moment that the average fishermen can make perhaps 400 casts with a deep crankbait in an 8 hour period. If each cast is 50 yards, and the bait spends 1/3 of that distance in the strike zone, the total productive distance covered in the period is something close to 6000 yards. A skilled fisherman trolling the same crankbait can cover that distance in little over an hour. From the perspective of High Percentage Fishing, I like that math. Much like live bait fishing, effective trolling is an art form that requires significant effort to hone the skill. In my opinion, it should be a part of every fisherman's arsenal of tactics. If you ignore or shun trolling you are leaving large numbers of fish out of the boat and perhaps even a few trophies.

There is complete agreement on the importance of anchoring in the world of big bass. First, anchoring allows high probability holding areas of big bass to be thoroughly worked with live bait or artificial lures. Secondly, anchoring maximizes the angler's ability to present to big fish in a stealthy noiseless fashion. The caveat, of course, is the importance of being confident you are fishing an area that is holding big fish. You cannot catch fish that are not there. This was one of the reasons Murphy was an advocate for becoming an expert on one or two lakes as opposed to fishing a larger number. The knowledge and confidence required to consistently find big fish is generally only acquired through concentration of effort in learning a body of water. I believe that developing the patience to position fish is one of the biggest challenges most anglers face in their hunt for big fish. You'll do yourself some favors if you set aside some time in the coming fishing season to give this approach a try.

In closing out this chapter, it should be noted, that all three of our big bass hunters fished warm southern waters. Some of their observations made on big bass behavior will have less application in cooler northern lakes and rivers with more dramatic seasonal changes. For instance, the general agreement on small home ranges for big bass may in large part be due to warm fertile waters of the south. Predator fish prioritize their biological needs as follows, oxygen, prey, security. Finding all three of these in abundance, fish may have little reason to relocate throughout the year. In northern water, basic seasonal changes may limit one critical factor or another and force fish to relocate, potentially over larger distances to meet their biological requirements.

Big Bass Profile

Big bass, those fish over 7lbs, behave very differently than small bass. Few if any male bass make it past 6lbs, so virtually all trophy bass are female. As apex predators in many bodies of water, they will lay territorial claims to lake locations that can sustain them year round with minimal movement. It is for this reason, large bass typically have small home ranges that rarely exceed a quarter mile in diameter in fertile lakes. Large bass feed aggressively and heavily, but primarily at dawn, dusk, and during the night. When not feeding the bass often suspend out in open water and are virtually uncatchable. These fish frequently use funnel points to move between offshore resting locations and shallower hunting grounds. All but the most extreme weather changes have little impact on their daily feeding habits. They are extremely sensitive to fishing pressure, and can become skittish or unapproachable if alerted to nearby fishermen.

Small Bass Profile

Small bass, those under 7lbs, are aggressive feeders who often actively hunt for as many as 20 hours per day. While they can be found throughout the three primary layers, many prefer the shallow layer as prey there tends to be smaller and more abundant. These fish tend to occupy less ideal locations on the lake that frequently cannot support year round residency. As a result, they typically have ranges that are several times the size of larger fish. More than bigger fish, they will move around to follow movements of baitfish. They are also more prone to be negatively influenced by weather.

Bass Biology

*"There he stands, draped in more equipment than a telephone
lineman, trying to outwit an organism with a brain no bigger
than a breadcrumb, and getting licked in the process."*
– Paul O'Neil

Basic Bass Biology

Weather, light levels, water temperature, availability of food, fishing pressure, habitat, and reproductive urges all influence bass behavior in a complicated web that could provide a lifetime of study for anglers. Many of these factors can themselves be quite variable, which further adds to the complexity. Before we begin our study of when and how each of these factors influence catch rates, it is first important to understand these fundamental drivers of bass behavior. For those looking for more detailed information for additional study, one of the best books I've come across on this topic is *"Knowing Bass, The Scientific Approach to Catching More Fish"* 2002, by Keith Jones, Ph.D.

Food

Bass are genetically programmed to eat. Left to their own devices, bass prefer small fish, crustaceans, and insects as their primary forage[1]. The process for determining what is or is not food is quite different than the thought process a human might go through. When presented with food, a human might consider factors such as where the food came from, how trustworthy is the source, how is it likely to taste, is it nutritious? After mentally assessing all of these factors a human will then take small tentative bites to test for agreeable tastes and textures before consuming the entire food item. Bass do not have this luxury. Their food is perpetually trying to escape them. In most cases they have only a fraction of a second to determine whether an item is or is not a prey item. Vast spans of time have left the fish with strong instincts that help them identify and consume prey. These instincts come in the form of mental models in the fishes' brain that determine whether an item is or is not food. Flashes of light, sound, vibration, smell, taste, movement; all these things are combined in the bass's brain and are processed in a fraction of a second. Fortunately, for us anglers, not every box in the bass's mental model must be checked to trigger a strike. An example of this is the spinnerbait. A spinnerbait does not closely resemble any prey a bass might encounter in its natural environment. However, a spinnerbait does emit flashes of light, vibration, and movement that check enough boxes in the bass's brain to convince it to strike[2]. It's important to note that not all strikes are motivated by the need for predation. Some strikes may be out of curiosity, reflex, or even an outward display of internal aggression[3]. A key to High Percentage Fishing is understanding current conditions and correctly identifying baits and presentations that are likely to combine with these external factors to create enough stimuli in the correct form to lead to a strike.

HP Tip: Mastering presentation techniques with a few high percentage lures is a statistically dominant strategy over the ability to present a wide variety of baits in an average fashion.

Vison

Vision is the primary sense used by bass to catch prey. It is important for High Percentage Fishermen to understand the basics of bass vision so they can apply these lessons in the best possible way to exploit the bass's weaknesses when it comes to vision. Bass have excellent vision, particularly at close range. In perfectly clear conditions, bass can probably see about 50 feet[4]. While we can't know the exact extent of the bass's ability to see objects outside the water, for those of us who have ever had a lure engulfed a moment before it hits the water we can be sure bass are able to see and are aware of the goings on beyond their watery domain. Doug Hannon, the "Bass Professor" went so far as to camouflage his boat, and deliberately kept a physically low profile while fishing in the belief that it improved his catch rates. To be sure the depth of the bass you are fishing for will dictate to some degree how sensitive the fish are to objects above the surface. Hannon primarily fished shallow water, so visual stealth was undoubtedly of more importance to him than another fisherman dragging a Carolina rig across deep structure. The strength of a bass's eyes lies in the transitioning shadow world of dawn and dusk[5]. During daylight hours, minnows and most other small prey have a significant eyesight advantage over bass. However as light levels begin to change, bass's eyes adjust to the change faster than their prey fish, thus giving the predator an advantage. This is one of the natural drivers that make low light conditions peak periods for bass fishing. At night, bass can see silhouettes but obviously rely on sight to a lesser degree. Fishing low light periods also plays to the fisherman's advantage. Not only are bass on the move, but the low light conditions also help disguise the fisherman and the lure they are using. As light levels decrease, the margin for error as it relates to lure presentation increases giving an advantage to the angler. When it comes to large bass, live bait presentations can significantly out produce artificial lures during bright daylight hours. Plainly, it can be difficult to fool a lunker with an artificial lure during this period. However, as light levels begin to drop, the advantage of live bait begins to fade and artificial lures begin to dominate because they are more forgiving to cast and can cover more water than live bait.

As it pertains to lure size, it is true that bigger baits generally yield bigger bass. However, if you are fishing for numbers, bass tend to be far more forgiving of downsizing lures than upsizing[6]. For High Percentage Fishermen, it is important to know the average size of fish in a given body of water. If you are fishing for numbers in a lake full of two-pound bass, you will be doing yourself a significant disservice throwing an 8" power worm. As a good rule of thumb, famed trophy hunter Bill Murphy typically started with plastic worms in the 5"-6" range. Based on the responses of fish, he would increase or decrease size as needed to yield the most bites. Generally speaking, larger lures yield better responses later in the year when summer's bounty has had a chance to increase the average forage size across the biomass.

As far as color goes, there is truth in the old adage of matching the hatch. However, when the color of local forage is unknown there are some general color guidelines that can be adopted for High Percentage Fishing. Studies from the Berkley Fish Research Data Bank have shown two toned lures (dark on top light on bottom) tend to out produce all other colors[7]. Think of the silver and black coloring on old standby Rapala's. Additionally, it's a good rule of thumb to stick with lighter colors in clear water or lighter days, and darker colors in stained water or on darker days. We will have more to say on color later when we examine the catch data.

Finally, we must spend some time addressing the way motion is perceived by bass. The motion of lures aids in selling the illusion of a prey item. Generally speaking, bass won't hit a lure they have not seen move[8]. Starts and stops or changes in speed can be particularly effective methods for High Percentage Fishermen to increase strikes per hour. The erratic motion may imitate the movement of an injured bait fish or simply differentiate your lure from hundreds of others the fish may have seen. One word of caution, just as in a new dating relationship, a little spontaneity can be attractive, but too much erratic behavior just comes across as crazy. Crazy can actually reduce strike rates. Add in low light levels along with purposeful changes in the cadence of moving baits and you've created a recipe for a highly effective lure that can easily fool bass into biting.

HP Tip: When in doubt about color selection remember the wisdom of Henry Ford's model Ts. Throw any color you like as long as it's black.

Taste and Smell

As we have discussed, bass primarily feed by sight. However, there are a few key concepts High Percentage Fishermen need to be in tune with when it comes to the sense of taste and smell in bass. In the bass's world of taste and smell, there are really just two sides of the coin to be considered. On one side we have scent attractors and on the other taste and smell deterrents.

There are many folks who swear scent attractors improve their fishing. There are others who argue they have no impact at all. I've used scent attractors for years and have closely monitored strike rates as compared to fellow fishermen in my boat. In the interest of transparency, I will admit this has not been a scientific study with any sort of formality in the usual sense of data collection. Additionally, I have searched far and wide but have been unable to locate an independent yet sizable data set that provides a statistically significant sample size to settle the debate once and for all. Now with that disclosure out of the way, I can say with a high degree of personal confidence that scent attractors in the world of bass fishing make very little difference in terms of catch rates. First, most chemical attractors are fairly expensive, setting a high bar for their practical use. That is to say, we should see a significant improvement in catch rates to justify their use. Next, most chemical attractors disperse fairly slowly. On fast moving hard bodied baits they offer virtually no advantage at all. In fact, they may be washed off the majority of their scent when they strike the water, leaving attractor where the bait was, not where it is. In terms of soft bodied baits, if you are planning to spend a great deal of time fishing a small area very slowly some slight advantage may develop. Saturation of the area with scent may attract fish to the area or trigger changes in the bass's brain that may shift a bass's mood into one more conducive to feeding. Additionally, studies by Berkley and other labs have shown conclusively that bass will hold onto scented baits longer, thus increasing the chance anglers can detect bites and successfully set the hook. For those curious, worm extract has been shown to be a favorite taste of bass[9]. In all, I would suggest scented baits have a slightly positive impact on catch rates, particularly during times you are fishing soft plastics slow and methodically through known bass haunts. Are they worth the additional expense? That's up to you as the angler to determine. Their most significant impact may, in fact, come from the ability to help mask other odors which act as a deterrent.

Deterrents are tastes or smells that bass find unpleasant which can lower catch rates either through fewer strikes or decreased hold time. When determining which compounds may be most worrisome, it is important to understand how bass taste and smell. Bass can taste only chemicals that are soluble in water[10]. The corollary in our world would be to attempt to suck water into our noses to try to smell. You would wind up with a whole lot of irritation and not a lot of smelling. Therefore, items like gasoline and engine oil are unlikely to have much of an impact on catch rates, simply because they are not water soluble. (Not that I'd recommend washing your hands in engine oil before you hit the water.) Other common items, however, can have a very detrimental impact on catch rates. Chief amongst them are bug sprays. Deet, a common chemical found in many insect repellents since the late 1950s has been shown to repel bass perhaps more so than mosquitoes! Studies have shown the detrimental impact on lures can last up to 90 minutes[11]. Sunscreen, detergents, and even human scent can also have negative effects, although their impact on fish is significantly lower than deet. In terms of advice for High Percentage Fishermen, I would strongly recommend avoiding bug spray to whatever extent possible. Finally, if you are concerned about other odor-deterrents, such as human scent or tobacco you may be wise to use an attractant spray to help mask the scent much as a hunter would, to reduce any negative effects.

HP Tip: There is a variety of performance wear geared toward fishermen on the market today. Many offer near full skin coverage made with breathable materials that can actually keep you cooler than if you were wearing shorts and t-shirt. Additionally, full coverage clothing does a significantly better job in protecting anglers from harmful UV radiation than sunscreen which could also potentially act as a scent deterrent when transferred from the hands to lures.

Hearing

In the hunt for prey, hearing takes the back seat to visual cues in the bass's world. Naturally, though, the lower the water visibility the more prominent a role hearing plays in locating prey. Sound travels 4.3 times faster in water than in air. Therefore, water is an excellent conductor of sound. In the ocean, whales have been confirmed to hear sounds from other whales from as far as a thousand miles away. It is undeniable that sound plays a critical role in helping bass locate potential prey from some distance. In addition to traditional auditory receptors we would call ears, bass also have a lateral line. The lateral line on bass works by detecting the movement of water molecules. While this sixth sense can play a critical role in bass predation, its range is limited to perhaps a little more than 3-4 feet around the bass[12]. Some studies have indicated that in clear water, noisy baits can actually reduce catch rates. Noise making lures are also amongst the easiest for caught bass to hold negative associations with. This phenomenon has been observed in many lakes, when noise/vibration making lures such as spinnerbaits, have had phenomenal catch rates when first introduced to a body of water, only to see them drop dramatically as fish become accustomed to the noise and vibration made by the lure. A corollary is the less pressure a body of water gets, the higher the likelihood sound may have a positive impact on catch rates. We've talked previously about pauses and changing the speed of retrieves to help trigger reaction bites from visual stimulus. The same is true for sound, not only does erratic sound help to trigger strikes, but it also helps to keep bass from becoming accustomed to the noise specific baits make. High Percentage Fishermen should therefore carefully consider adding noise makers to their lures. If water clarity is sufficient to allow bass to hunt visually, adding noise makers to lures may be more of a liability than an asset.

Ken Smith, in his 2013 article *"Double Digits, It Can Happen to You"* relayed a story about an encounter he had with John Hope in the early 1990s. In the story, Ken tells that he was invited along to join Hope while he was tracking a large 15 lb. fish they had tagged on Lake Fork in East Texas. The fish had a home territory on a run of the mill secondary point of which there are hundreds on Lake Fork. Ken even identified the location of the fish, (32°50.780N and 95°34.862W) to help drive home the point that big bass do not operate like the Loch Ness Monster occupying haunts in the deepest darkest depths of the lake. One cypress tree, in particular, was a common location for the fish to suspend in about 12 feet of water. As Hope approached the location in the boat, he killed the engine about 150 yards away from the cypress tree. He then instructed all the occupants of the boat to be perfectly quiet. He positioned the boat so that the wind gently blew the boat within 10 yards of the cypress tree and then past about another 150 yards or so. The entire time they monitored the fish and noted it did not move from its suspended location adjacent to the cypress. Firing up the big motor, they circled around for another pass. This time, Hope flipped on his fish finder. After only drifting a few yards, the trophy fish swam off from the cypress in the opposite direction. They never got closer than 80 yards to the fish. Hope noted that similar reactions occurred with a variety of boat noise including trolling motors and the sound of noisy anglers. One minor exception of note was that on occasion they were able to approach big fish with the trolling motor on constant. However, cycling trolling motors on and off he noted was a dead giveaway that virtually always put big fish on the move.

HP Tip: Do not use your fish finder unless you absolutely have to. Many anglers have become accustomed to flipping on their units, even on lakes they know like the back of their hands. The use of fish finders should not be viewed as a "free activity" there is a potential cost associated with their use in terms of lower catch rates, particularly of larger fish.

Feel/Temp

Of all the environmental factors, temperature probably has the biggest impact on bass behavior. Being cold-blooded creatures, the temperature of the water around bass dictates many of their biological functions. These range from location in the lake to their current metabolic rate, which in turn dictates how often fish must feed. The preferred temperature range for bass is between 80 and 90 degrees Fahrenheit[13]. That said, the importance of temperature to bass, is a relative factor dependent upon the temperature they are currently in. To a bass in 40-degree water, there is perhaps no greater biological drive than to find the warmest water it can in its preferred layer. The warmer water will increase the speed and responsiveness of the bass's muscles giving them an advantage over many prey species that experience similar, but smaller positive changes in muscle movement. However, the importance of temperature has its limits. To a bass in 70-degree water, seeking warmer water may take a backseat to other factors such as availability of cover, prey, and maintaining distance from boating and fishing pressure[14]. As can be seen in the figure below, many of the common prey species have preferred temperatures that are far lower than that of largemouth bass. A bass might be completely cozy in 90-degree water, but its high metabolic rate will demand it eats regularly and it may find prey extremely scarce at those temperatures. Bass rarely position themselves in places they do not have ready access to adequate food sources.

Freshwater Baitfish	*Prefered Temp* (Degrees F)
Lake Chub	45-55
Gold Fish	77
Northern Hog Sucker	50+
Killfishes	85
Bluntnose Minnow	84
Fathead Minnow	84
Sculpins	45-55
Gizzard Shad	63-80
Threadfin Shad	71-75
Common Shiner	65-83
Emerald Shiner	61-72
Goloden Shiner	70
Spotfin Shiner	80s
Spottail Shiner	54
Mountain Sucker	60-74

In addition to positioning of bass and prey species, water temperature also dictates another biological imperative for fish; oxygen levels. Particularly in warm water seasons, oxygen levels can be one of the best overall predictors of fish location. In many bodies of water, thermoclines will set up. Thermoclines are a naturally developing layer in the water column that separates cold water on the bottom of a lake from warm water on the surface. Below the thermocline, water will be virtually devoid of oxygen creating a biological no man's land for fish. Considering these layers very often develop between the 15-25 foot ranges, vast portions of many lakes can be eliminated as potential holding areas for fish. Above the thermocline, generally speaking, the warmer the water the lower the amount of oxygen it contains. This further aids anglers in pinning down the position of bass. Fish in warm water have oxygen requirements that are far higher than bass in cooler water. The lesson here, for High Percentage Fishermen, is that the likely holding areas of bass can be pinned down comparatively easily, particularly during the summer, simply by excluding those areas of the lake that have insufficient oxygen levels to support numbers of bass.

HP Tip: Wind action and photosynthesis from green vegetation are two primary methods oxygen enters the water in the summer. Conversely, the biological process of rotting organic material consumes oxygen and releases carbon dioxide. Therefore, during warm water periods areas of lakes that contain large amounts of rotting organic material, like stump fields, may be too oxygen-poor to support large numbers of fish even though they provide fantastic cover. However, wind driving into a stump field or grass beds amongst the wood may create a perfect combination cover and oxygen that harbors large numbers of fish.

References:

1. Keith A. Jones Ph.D., Knowing Bass, The Scientific Approach to Catching More Fish The Lyons Press, 2002), 14.
2. Ibid., 15.
3. Ibid., 16.
4. Ibid., 152.
5. Ibid., 154.
6. Ibid., 175.
7. Ibid., 181.
8. Ibid., 167.
9. Ibid., 57.
10. Ibid., 85.
11. Ibid., 111.
12. Ibid., 15.
13. Ibid., 196.
14. Ibid., 228.

Fishing Pressure

"The gods do not deduct from man's allotted span the hours spent in fishing." – Babylonian Proverb

I'm going to start this section with a bold and potentially contentious statement: **Fishing pressure is the single greatest causal factor influencing catch rates**. Stated another way, the more recently and the heavier a lake has been fished, the lower catch rates will be. This is true for several reasons. First, on days with heavy pressure, it becomes increasingly difficult to fish high percentage spots at peak times. We've all experienced it before; there are few things more depressing than to motor around a point to your favorite spot only to find two other boats already sitting there. Secondly, I firmly believe heavy fishing and boating pressure slows the bite. Perhaps it's the motor noise, the incessant pings of hundreds of depth finders, or the never ending procession of lures swimming by. Whatever the cause, catch rates decline in the face of heavy pressure. Lastly, when a lot of people fish, a lot of fish get caught. When a bass gets hooked the odds of that fish biting again, particularly over the next several hours, drops dramatically. This is a bit of an elementary exercise in mathematics, but let's use a hypothetical Lake X to illustrate the point. On a particular day let's say Lake X has 1000 bass that are actively feeding. Of those bass, about 1/3 of them are in the deep layer, 1/3 of them are in the middle layer, and 1/3 of them are in the shallow layer. Since the vast majority of bass fishermen focus on waters 8 feet and less we can say that at most 300-400 bass are catchable on this particular day. Naturally if there are 100 boats, on average each boat is likely to catch something like 3-4 bass. Sure, some will catch many more, some will get skunked, but on average it's likely to shake out to a few bass per boat. Conversely, if there are only 10 boats on the lake each boat might catch as many as 30-40 bass. While there are obviously some basic assumptions that are made in this model, it leads us to a very important law of fishing. Given a lake that typically has fishing pressure X, catch rates will change in a linear fashion. That is to say, if a lake typically has 100 boats on it on any given Saturday, all other things laid equal, your catch rates will likely be 10% higher if you arrive on a Saturday and there are only 90 boats on the lake.

After reviewing tens of thousands of data points related to catch rates, one single factor stands out over all other environmental factors with day to day variability: pressure. Virtually all fishermen are aware of the negative effects of pressure, but for the most part this variable is largely ignored. Other factors such as wind direction and barometric pressure get far more scrutiny than fishing pressure. The data tells a different story, fishing pressure is the single most important environmental factor High Percentage Fishermen should consider on any given outing.

Fishing pressure comes in three primary forms. First there is a selective pressure. This is the genetic pressure that occurs on a species as its environment changes over time. Second there is general pressure. This is the pressure that occurs from the presence of people on or in the aquatic environment. The third type of pressure is the fishing pressure that occurs directly as a result of man's attempt to catch fish via hook and line.

Selective Pressure

For millions of years, fish on this planet existed without the presence of man. Their only concerns in life were food, safety, and reproduction. While perhaps sounding ideal, nature is coldly indifferent. It molds species through a daily life and death drama that has played out across the entire globe for eons. Species genetically change slowly over successive generations through selective environmental pressures. For any life with DNA, genetic mutations occur during the DNA replication process, which is a biologic process that occurs in all species. In the vast majority of cases, these changes have little or no noticeable effect on the individual creature. Sometimes the mutations can be highly deleterious causing deformities or defects that can cause the animal to have a difficult time surviving. Other times, perhaps rarest of all, mutations can have a positive effect on the survival of the species.

Imagine for instance that we had two large lakes completely isolated in a remote corner of the earth. One has primary cover that exists in the form of rocks, and the other has primary cover that exists in the form of weeds. Now imagine that millions of years ago we released a few thousand silver bass like creatures into each of these bodies of water. We know from biologists, a large female may lay up to 40,000 eggs in a nest. Studies have shown, however, that less than two-tenths of one percent might survive their first year. A mere 80 fish out of 40,000! Some die from environmental factors such as water temperature or starvation, still others fall prey to hungry predators. As each successive year passes, this cycle continues over and over again. Fish are born, most die, but a very few survive to pass along their genes to their offspring. With such large numbers in play over vast periods of time, we might expect that even a small advantage might be hugely beneficial in terms of survival. What might we expect to find if we looked at that same lake today? It is very likely that if we looked in the lake with rock cover, we would find fish that might look very much like modern day smallmouth whose bronze color blends in nicely in a rocky environment. Similarly, if we looked in the lake with weeds as primary cover, we might find fish that look strikingly like our modern day largemouth. Over long periods of time fish that were born with colorings that varied from their silver parents, perhaps a slight brownish color, for example, might have had a far better chance of surviving because they more closely blended into the surrounding environment thus making it more difficult for predators to locate them. This would, in turn, increase their chance of reaching reproductive age and thus spread the "brown" gene to their offspring. Most folks acknowledge that adaptation in animals on at least small scales, such as changes in coloration, can occur over time. Coming to terms with this type change is important for High Percentage Fishermen because it allows us to see how our fishing reality might be changing over time due to new survival pressures man has introduced into aquatic environments.

As fishing pressure increases, those fish which have genetic makeups that make them less susceptible to angling have a far greater chance of survival. For instance, those that are better able to discern that artificial lures are not food are less likely to be hooked and less likely to suffer an injury which might lead to death. This aversion to lures will then be passed down to their offspring and as the cycle continues it is conceivable that an entire population of bass might become exceedingly difficult to catch by conventional methods. In all probability, this process has already begun in some of our lakes today! Make no mistake, man's presence is an environmental factor that has changed and will continue to change bass as time marches on.

People Pressure

The second form of pressure is people pressure. That is to say simply the presence of people on a body of water. In today's world, the presence of people on lakes is hardly discrete. If you've ever been on a popular body of water in the summer, you know exactly what I'm talking about. Lakes may be so overridden with pleasure boats and various sport craft that it can be difficult for anyone to enjoy the water, let alone a fish who actually lives in that water! I fully believe that fish can become conditioned to drastically reduce daytime activity levels on lakes that are experiencing heavy pressure. Whether this is a genetic trait passed down over generations (remember a single generation in bass years can be as little as one year,) or simply a learned behavior, bass hunker down and are far more difficult to catch on heavily pressured lakes. Compounding matters, fishing lakes swarming with pleasure boaters can be nearly impossible due to wave action, which makes lure presentation and bite detection exceedingly difficult.

Fishing Pressure

Finally, the third form of pressure is pressure we are perhaps all most familiar with; angling pressure. A key advantage to fishing shallow is that an angler maximizes the time his lure is in the strike zone. By their nature most lures are more easily fished in shallow water. Once a lure touches the water it must descend to the desired level, run at the level, and then ascend back to the angler. When fishing a topwater lure, the lure is in the desired strike zone (the surface of the water) nearly 100% of a cast. Fished slowly, a Texas rigged worm may spend as much as 80% of a cast in the strike zone. Deep diving crankbaits may only spend 30% of total cast length at the target depth. For most lures, the deeper it is fished the less time the lure spends at the target depth. Said another way, the deeper one fishes the more precise the presentation must be, simply because the time the lure spends in the strike zone is dramatically lower than when fishing shallow water. This is one of the primary reasons most bass fishermen spend their time fishing shallow water. Some angling studies indicate that bass fishermen spend as much as 90% of their time fishing water 8 feet or less. This places an enormous amount of pressure on shallow water fish.

Fish that have been recently caught are significantly less likely to bite than fish that have not been recently caught. This is a very simple concept, but it has profound implications far beyond what most anglers consider on a given outing. Imagine for a moment that you hit the water on a Monday morning and head straight to your favorite spot. You fish for a few hours, but nothing bites and you ultimately wind up heading home, frustrated once again by the mysterious nature of your quarry. You chalk the whole debacle up to low barometric pressure, high barometric pressure, the wrong moon phase, the wrong lure color, or wind from whichever direction. The reality of the matter, however, is that unbeknownst to you there was a large fishing tournament the day before. The spot was hit hard all day long by a procession of anglers; the early birds of which did quite well in the spot! No wonder you didn't catch any fish from the area. As a fish, you don't have to be an aquatic Einstein to know better than to hit another lure when you still have a sore mouth from the last one. Yes, it happens that the same fish have been caught repeatedly in short periods of time, but from a probability point of view, most bass are less likely to strike lures when they've recently been caught.

Fishermen can also pressure fish with lures. To various degrees, studies have shown that bass can learn. They may not learn in the same way that you and I think of the word, but they can learn to associate certain stimuli with negative experiences. This is particularly true for noise making lures. The less natural a lure is in form, texture, or noise, the higher the probability that bass, particularly large fish will have negative associations with it. Spinnerbaits, for instance, make a very distinctive noise that can make them less productive baits over time in waters where they are heavily fished. We will explore this matter further in the big bass lure chapter, but let me drop a hint and say that soft plastic baits are one of the few subsets of lures that do not seem to show significant drops in catch rates over extended periods of time. They are natural enough that fish seem unable to learn that they are potentially dangerous.

How to Combat Selective Pressure

Selective pressure is a complex problem to solve. I am not sure that any one solution fully addresses all concerns. In the days of old when it was common to harvest virtually every fish an angler caught, the problem was particularly pronounced. Those fish with a higher proclivity to bite artificial lures were quickly caught and removed from the gene pool leaving only those fish with a genetic makeup that made them more difficult to catch. The rise of catch and release eased this problem but created another in the form of lakes filled with fish that were well educated to the ploys of fishermen. Minimizing the negative effects of pressure, both selective and otherwise, is a worthy field of study that we would do well as a group to support in the coming decades. Failure to do so could leave our children with lakes full of fish that are hard to find and even harder to catch. Fortunately, in terms of boating and fishing pressure, High Percentage Fishermen can control their own fates by strategically picking the best places and times to minimize the negative effects of pressure.

Combating General Pressure

The best approach to minimizing the impact of general pressure is to pick the place and time you are going to fish. Most folks have jobs and do not have unlimited flexibility on when they get to fish. However, virtually all of us have quite a bit more flexibility than we might think. Nowhere is it written that all fishing must occur on the weekend during the day. In fact, the data tells us scheduling your outings in this fashion has a hugely negative impact on catch rates. As a High Percentage Fisherman, I go to great lengths to try to plan my outings to places and during times where general pressure is likely to be minimized. If I am planning to head to a particular lake in a given week, I'll first think about any extenuating circumstances that might drive up pressure beyond normal levels. Are there any holidays? Are there any tournaments scheduled? I'll scour the internet to check. I'm of the opinion, that large tournaments are perhaps the single worst sort of pressure a lake can receive. Not only does it max out general pressure, but it also maxes out fishing pressure. There are few conditions an angler will encounter worse than fishing a lake right after a large number of skilled anglers have just pounded it for multiples days. Avoid fishing during and directly after tournaments if at all possible. In the case of large tournaments on comparatively small lakes, it might take weeks for lakes to return to normal catch rates. Once I have narrowed the dates for my outing down to a particular day or two based on anticipated pressure, I'll then begin to consider weather and other factors. As we will see in a few chapters, low light periods around morning and dusk are best. The earlier and later you fish, typically the lower the overall pressure. Do not forget about night fishing. Night fishing is becoming increasingly popular, but in some extreme cases, it may be one of the few ways left that anglers can still experience solid catch rates on extremely pressured lakes.

Combating Fishing Pressure

Once you have selected the day and the time of your outing, the next step becomes making an assessment of the likely fishing pressure and using this information to develop your strategy for the day. The higher the fishing pressure the greater the need to look for areas of the lake that are likely to receive lower pressure. The vast majority of anglers are going to stick to fishing areas that are easy to access and easy to fish. In most cases this is going to mean obvious easy to reach shallow water cover. In cases where I'm fishing virgin water or water that generally receives very low pressure, these easy to find locations are the exact areas I target! As pressure increases, however, you must become more resourceful to maintain catch rates. This will mean looking for bass in areas other anglers don't. In the shallows, this can mean thick cover that is a hassle to get at or a hassle to fish. More generally this could mean deeper water. As we have seen from John Hope, fish use all three portions of the water column, yet anglers primarily focus on shallow water. Fishing deep water is not easy. If it were easy, everyone would do it and it wouldn't be a low-pressure area. Fortunately, the secrets of the deep are becoming increasingly easy to access. Deepwater crankbaits are probing depths never before touched by lures and modern day electronics are vastly superior to those available to previous generations. Much of this may seem very elementary, but it is the single most important factor you can control on any given outing. It is advice that is widely ignored. If you don't believe me, go to any given boat ramp across the country and count the number of trailers at the ramp at 6 a.m. versus the number at 8 a.m. You'll quickly see that what some may consider common sense, isn't so common.

Section 2

The Data

Piscemetrics

"Many men fish their entire lives without realizing it's not the fish they are after." – Henry David Thoreau

In northern climates during the coldest of the hard water months, there exists a ubiquitous phenomenon amongst passionate anglers joking called "winternet." The shine of ice fishing has faded for many, yet long months lay ahead before the first baits can be cast. It is during this time that fishermen head in droves to one of the few places north of the 42nd parallel where their desire for all things fishing can be readily fed; the internet. It was just such a period in 2012, having wandered endlessly on the web, that I stumbled across a dataset of freshwater catch information that had been self-reported by anglers. Being familiar with statistics, I knew that small datasets with unverified information could be prone to reporting error. That is to say, if you have a hundred data points and 10% of the data was unwittingly faulty it would be very easy to draw erroneous conclusions. Since I had no way to guarantee the validity of the data I knew the only way I could statistically draw conclusions was if I had a much larger sample size. So I continued my search, trying to gather more data to let the power of statistics begin to work its magic. Over time, I began to find additional datasets, some from clubs, some fishing organizations, others from statewide initiatives like the Texas ShareLunker Program. Slowly but surely I began piecing together a large dataset, some of which had been gathered and recorded for decades by thousands of anglers. Not all the data recorded the same variables, but in many cases the same basic information was available, such as date, time, catch size, water temperature, and lure choice. In all, I wound up with data on more than 40,000 individual catches tied directly to freshwater predator fishing in North America.

Educated as an Engineer and a Lean Six Sigma Black Belt, these datasets were tantamount to discovering a buried treasure in my backyard. In my profession, Six Sigma is concerned with the use of statistical tools to identify causal factors in manufacturing to minimize variation in production processes. I discovered I could apply the same statistical tools I used in my profession to identify which casual variables in the catch data seemed to have the biggest impact on fishing. I spent weeks pouring over the data, slicing and dicing it every imaginable way. What improved catch rates? Was it the time of day? Was it lure selection? Lure color? To be sure I made some interesting discoveries about which baits seemed to catch the most fish and which lakes were the most prolific producers, but nothing I discovered seemed to be a game changer. One of the big weaknesses of the data I had stitched together was it very often did not include weather data. Conversely, if it did include weather data it did not seem reliably recorded. As we all know, fishermen are bad enough at accurately reporting catch sizes, let alone weather conditions at the time of the catch. So I sat on the data over the next year as I pondered how I might extract more meaningful insights. Then one week I was looking at weather websites trying to decide which day of the upcoming week to fish. While perusing the website I noticed they offered a service that allowed anyone to download historic weather data for essentially any zip code in the US for a reasonable fee. This observation flipped a switch in my mind. If I added this reliable weather information to my stockpile of detailed catch data I might be able to make some more actionable observations.

Much of what is written in this section is the result of analyzing tens of thousands of catch data points combined with detailed hourly information on weather, solar, and lunar conditions from regions as far south as Texas to as far north as Ontario. In the world of baseball, the application of statistical tools in an effort to improve the outcome of games is called

Sabermetrics. The concept has been wildly successful for many ball clubs, and was dramatized in the popular movie, "Moneyball." I like to think similar strategies can be applied to fishing to improve catch rates. The Latin word for fish is "Pisces," so perhaps this field would be called, "Piscemetrics." This section outlines my findings using Piscemetrics to try to find High Percentage Fishing approaches to improve catch rates. Some of you may find you disagree with certain concepts, others may find they align nicely with your own mental models; my hope is that all will find something that helps you become a better fisherman.

Weather

"Fishing is a discipline in the equality of men – for all men are equal before fish." – Herbert Hoover

Air Pressure

Barometric pressure is perhaps the most widely discussed weather related predictor of fishing success. In fact, one of the primary drivers for beginning my data analysis was to try to confirm the popular fishing adage that dropping barometric pressure positively influences the feeding behavior of bass. A widespread theory on this matter is that dropping air pressure causes a decrease in water pressure, which in turn causes underwater organisms to rise in the water column. Conversely, as pressure increases, organisms (especially plankton) are forced into vegetation and other areas where larger predators have a more difficult time reaching them.

For reference, at sea level mean barometric pressure pushes down with a force of approximately 14.7lbs per square inch. All organisms are accustomed this pressure so there is no perceived sensation of the force. Furthermore, a 1 millibar change in pressure equates to about .015lbs per square inch change in force. Generally, over the course of several hours pressure rarely shifts by more than a few millibars, so the actual change in force on any organism is minimal. Certainly not something that would be perceived by humans or noticeably impact the position of bass in the water column.

Before we dive into the data, there are a few important concepts related to atmospheric pressure we should cover. First of all, there is a common misconception that cold fronts are low pressure and warm fronts are high pressure. While it is true that cooling air drops its pressure and that heating it increases pressure there are a myriad of other factors that play into whether a particular mass of air is low or high pressure. Most notably among these aspects is that pressure regions are measured relative to other pressure regions around them.

There is no magic cut off on the barometric scale that makes a mass of air high or low pressure. It is for this reason that it is entirely possible for a warm mass of air to be low pressure in relation to a higher pressure cool mass of air and vice versa. If all this sounds confusing it is precisely one of the reasons why barometric pressure is a poor overall predictor of fishing success.

When reviewing the data, the basic statistical approach used was to stratify periods of time in 1, 3, 6, and 12 hour periods in which pressure went up or down. For instance, if pressure dropped over a 3 hour period it would be put into the decreasing pressure data bucket. Similarly, if pressure increased over a similar period it would go into the rising pressure category. Catch rates for each 1, 3, 6, and 12 hour period were then compared to the overall catch rate for the data set. Catch rates that were significantly higher or lower than the base catch rate would then indicate a variable of possible significance. **What the findings indicate first and foremost is that a great many fish are caught across the full spectrum of barometric pressure.** The graphs on the following page show the impact on catch rates over time. Interestingly, moderately decreasing or increasing pressure had no notable impact on catch rates. However, stable pressure significantly improved catch rates around the 12-hour mark. This indicates that stability in weather has far greater impact on catch rates than any normal changes in weather.

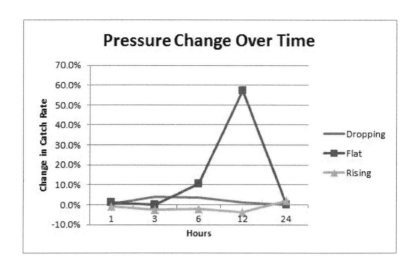

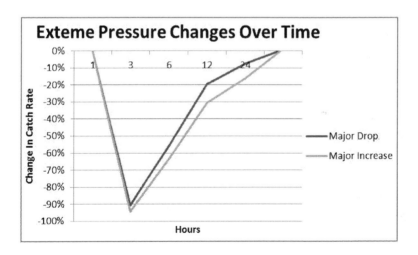

This is an important concept that High Percentage Fishermen should look for in weather forecasts when planning outings. The second graph shows how rapid changes in barometric pressure influenced catch rates. Categorically we can see that the bite does not "shut off" at high or low pressure, nor do catch rates significantly change given moderate increases or decreases in pressure. Only in the most extreme cases of rapidly increasing or decreasing pressure did bite rates seem to be negatively affected around the 3-hour mark after the onset of the change. These cases are rare in the data and are usually associated with the passage of a major storm or frontal system. Even in these cases, it is difficult to say with statistical certainty whether catch rates have been negatively impacted, simply because the passage of major frontal systems may cloak significantly reduced fishing effort as many fishermen avoid fishing in these conditions. After weeks of slicing and dicing the data in every imaginable way, **there was only one change in pressure that proved to be a statistically significant predictor of increased catch rates: stability**. Catch rates improved when pressure remained stable over time, or when pressure changed only slightly over time, which is really just an indicator of general stability. Intuitively this makes sense, stable pressure is indicative of stable weather which in turns allows fish to develop predictable feeding routines that can be patterned by fishermen, thus improving catch rates. **On the whole, barometric pressure has a far lower impact on fishing than most anglers attribute to it.** Fish are regularly caught across nearly the full spectrum of "normal" barometric conditions. The real question anglers should be asking is not whether the pressure is low or high, decreasing or increasing, but how stable has the weather been?

HP Tip: One of the best weather websites I have found is www.weatherspark.com. It provides a wealth of historic and forecasted weather data from a variety of sources.

Warm/Cold Fronts

As we have seen previously, fish are sensitive to water temperature changes. It's for this reason that warming and cooling, particularly at certain times of the year have a more noticeable impact on fishing than barometric pressure. Water temperature changes more slowly than surface air temperatures, but anglers should be mindful that even several hours of cooler or warmer air temperatures can influence surface water temperature by as much as a couple of degrees. With few exceptions anglers should be mostly concerned about cooling trends. Cooling waters slow metabolism reducing the frequency of feeding and increasing the length of time required for digestion. Water temperature has a much more significant impact on catch rates than the barometric pressure in most cases.

Humidity

Humidity has no statistically significant impact on fishing catch rates.

Cloud Cover

When questioned on the matter, most fishermen would likely hypothesis that cloud cover, or perhaps more accurately stated- light levels, have a significant impact on fishing catch rates. As previously covered, baitfish have an advantage over bass in high light levels. As such we would expect to see improved catch rates on days with increased cloud cover, which reduces light levels and decreases the baitfish's advantage during the day. In analyzing the data, sky conditions were labeled as clear, partly cloudy, or overcast. Catch rates during each of these periods were then compared to the expected catch rate based on the frequency those sky conditions occurred. That is to say, if there were 100 catches over a period of time, and the sky was overcast 25% of that time, we would expect 25 of the 100 catches to have occurred during overcast conditions if cloud cover had no impact on catch rates. Catch rates higher than 25% during overcast skies would indicate that overcast conditions positively influenced catch rates while rates under 25% would indicate a negative impact. Surprisingly, in examining the data, the assumption that overcast conditions improve catch rates is shown to be false. Sunny and partly cloudy conditions significantly outperformed expected catch rates, by roughly 20% while overcast conditions underperformed by nearly as much. I've no clear explanation for why this counterintuitive outcome is occurring, but the sample size included over 10,000 catches and the result was statistically significant by a wide margin. One possible explanation is that overcasts skies reduce light levels giving bass an advantage over natural prey, thus reducing bites on artificial lures.

Rain

The data tells us that rain itself has no statistically significant impact on catch rates. Plenty of fish are caught in the rain. In fact, given that rain typically reduces fishing pressure, a compelling argument can be made that rain can actually indirectly improve catch rates. In general, I certainly wouldn't fear light rain. Where rain can become detrimental is when it has a substantial impact on water levels or water temperature. Cold rain can rapidly decrease water temperature which in turn can lower metabolic rates and thus the feeding frequency of bass. Heavy or prolonged rain can rapidly raise water levels and in reservoirs may significantly reduce visibility due to muddy water flowing in from feeder creeks. Particularly in the spring heavy rains can introduce a great deal of cold muddy water into a lake which can create some of the toughest fishing conditions an angler can encounter. The cold water slows metabolic rate, reduces feeding frequency, and the muddy water dramatically reduces the strike zone of fish further reducing catch rates. Compounding the situation, vast amounts of new water can disperse fish across a much wider area making locating fish a far more difficult task. Typically fish will push shallow into the new water capitalizing on the opportunistic feeding frenzy made possible by a deluge of insects and other organic material that has become newly submerged.

Wind

A review of wind's impact on catch rates was completed by comparing catch percentages during particular wind conditions with the overall frequency of that condition during the time period of the study. As an example, if wind did not impact catch rates, we would expect that catch percentages for a particular wind condition would match the percentage of time that condition existed. This would be our base case. If the percentage of catches were higher than the percentage of time the condition existed, that would be an indication of a positive causal factor. Conversely, if catch rates were significantly lower, it would be an indication of a negative impact. As can be seen in the graph below, the data tells us the wind is your friend. There are likely several reasons why catch rates improve with

Impact of Wind on Catch Rates

Condition	% of Catches	% of Time Condition Exists
Calm (0-3 mph)	20%	20%
Slight (3-8 mph)	45%	29%
Moderate (8-15 mph)	29%	25%
Strong (15 mph +)	6%	3%

wind. First, the wind creates waves which can oxygenate the water, which in turn can increase fish activity. Furthermore, wave action scatters light, which helps disguise the fact a lure is a lure. Finally, wave action helps conceal fishermen and their boats both visually and acoustically. All these factors combine to improve overall catch rates in the presence of wind as opposed to the calm condition. Perhaps most interestingly, catch rates were more than double the base rate for winds over 15 mph. Certainly these conditions can be tough even potentially dangerous to fish in, but they can also be very rewarding.

HP Tip: Strong winds driving into shallow water can create an environment uncomfortable for bass. Try pulling off normal fish holding locations into nearby structure in slightly deeper water that will be less disturbed by turbulent water.

Fog

Before this study, I would have assumed fog would have a positive association with catch rates. If nothing else, I suspected the lower light levels that come with fog would improve fishing. As it turns out, the fog seems to have no statistical impact on catch rates. Any advantage that comes with lower light levels could well be neutralized by the cooler air temperatures often associated with fog. One thing we can be sure of is that fog raises many safety issues on the water. Anglers would be well advised to consider whether the risks of fog outweigh the statistically non-existent rewards.

Moon Myths

"Too many fishermen are unknowingly handicapped because they have acquired a zealous belief in what they consider to be gospel-truth facts that are actually nothing more than myths."
— John Hope

Across all forms of fishing, there is a commonly held belief that lunar phases have an impact on the feeding cycles of fish. Widely published tables have developed over the years in an effort to predict these cycles and many times they draw on about as much scientific data as an astrologer. Perhaps nowhere is this correlation more pronounced than in the world of musky fishing. If there is one pointer most musky fishermen know it's that fishing moon rise and moon set, particularly around new and full moons are peak periods for boating fish. Popularized by Joe Bucher, this theory has been hotly debated but generally accepted by most musky anglers. Much like their northern counterparts, many bass anglers have also adopted a similar belief that the feeding habits of their quarry are largely influenced by a distant celestial body.

To complete this study, thousands of catch data points were examined across multiple species of freshwater predator fish and laboriously compared to detailed data on lunar cycles. Before we dive into the statistics let's have a brief discussion about the moon. Most folks have little trouble imagining how the moon might influence fishing either through its gravity or through the light it reflects. We've all seen tides and we've all been out on nights when the moon was so bright you could see with ease. There are perhaps other more exotic, almost magical theories folks might have as to how the moon might influence fish behavior. If you have these, I'd be interested to hear them and also interested in selling you some fairy dust you can dip your bait in. The stuff works great!

For the purposes of tackling this problem from a data-based scientific perspective, I've listed a few hypotheses for evaluation that might act as causal channels from the moon to influence fish behavior.

Gravity

We all know the moon is gravitationally tied to the earth. Ocean tides are the most notable manifestation of this phenomenon. I'm not going to diverge into a dissertation about how the moon drives tides, but if you are interested Google can quickly help you understand. The important takeaway for our discussion is that the gravitational pull of the moon drives tides but that bodies of water have to be *VAST* to have a notable tide. The largest non-ocean tides occur in the great lakes and at their peak amount to about 2 inches. Scientists generally consider them non-tidal. Smaller lakes, even the giant Lake of the Woods do not have measurable tides. Simply put, when you are fishing in freshwater, tides are not a factor. Furthermore, the actual gravitational pull of the moon on a large bass is about .0003 Newtons or .00006 lbs. It is an incredibly small force. To put it into perspective, **your boat has a stronger gravitational pull on a netted fish than the moon does!** Remember also that the pull of gravity from the moon does not substantially change given the position of the moon. It is true that gravity is *slightly* stronger when the moon is up, but only about 1.5% stronger; that's .000061 lbs of force. The largest changes in gravitational pull occur when the moon aligns with the sun (new moon) but even this change is still exceptionally small. So what is the minimum threshold of gravity a fish can feel? At present, no studies exist that answer this question, but what can be said with a high degree of certainty is that virtually everything in the fish's environment (waves, air pressure etc...) has a far greater influence on fish than the exceptionally small gravitational pull of the moon.

Hypothesis 1: *The moon's gravity affects fishing.*

Interestingly, the moon's orbit is not perfectly round, and as such its distance from the earth varies throughout the year. This allows us to easily check to see if the moon's gravity impacts fishing using the gravitational formula $F=Gm1*m2/(r^2)$. We can test this by checking to see if catch rates change based on the distance of the moon. If gravity levels play little or no role we should not see much statistical variation between catch rates during times of high gravity vs. low gravity.

Light Levels

We know light levels play a major role in fishing. We also know the moon can have a significant impact on light levels. Nights are very dark during new moons and much brighter during full moons. How this impacts fishing is difficult to say. Some studies suggest that full moons and the associated increase in nighttime light levels actually drive baitfish (and thus predator fish) deeper making them more difficult to catch. Others say the added light makes it easier for predators to locate fish at night and thus improves fishing. In either case, this is a testable relationship.

Hypothesis 2: *The moon's light levels impact fishing.*

This theory is fairly straightforward to test. If the level of reflected light from the moon matters, fishing should either improve or worsen based on brightness. If more light improves fishing then we should see increased catch rates around full moons. If more light decreases catch rates we should see a drop off in fishing around full moons. Naturally the inverse of this would also be true for new moons. If light levels play little or no role we should not see much statistical variation between new and full moons.

Position of the Moon

Even if gravity and reflected light prove to have no statistical link, perhaps there is something intangible beyond these factors that could affect the fishing. One such widely believed indicator is the position of the moon relative to the earth. Moon overhead and moon underfoot are often mentioned as a cause for initiating minor feed periods while moonrise and moonset are generally associated with major feeding cycles. Try as I might I have been unable to think of a way a fish might be aware, for instance, the moon is underfoot. But let's imagine for a moment some kind of magical moon ray that broadcasts the position of the moon. Given this, let's look at the indicator for major feeding cycles and test the theory that moonrise and moonset impact catch rates.

Hypothesis 3: *Moonrise and moonset improve fishing.*

This is also fairly straightforward to test. If this is the case, we would expect to see higher catch rates around moonset and moonrise. An important caveat here relates to new and full moons. New and full moons always set and rise very close to actual sunrise and sunset. (Check this for yourself if you don't believe me!) These are classic low light level conditions, which naturally produce more fish. Therefore, if moonrise and moonset do impact fishing, the best way to test this would be during partial moon phases when the rising and setting of the moon does not closely correlate to the rising and setting of the sun. In essence, we are removing an extra variable to ensure we are just testing our base hypothesis.

Findings

Hypothesis 1: *The moon's gravity affects fishing.*

Results: In the portion of the fishing season that the moon had it its peak gravitational impact (closest) 7.3% of all fish were caught. In the portion of the fishing season that the moon had its weakest gravitational impact (farthest) 9.0% of fish were caught. Given the sample size of the data collected, these two means are so close they do not turn out to be statistically significant. We reject our hypothesis. Therefore, we cannot say in any statistically relevant sense that the intensity of the moon's gravitational pull positively or negatively impacts catch rates. You're just as likely to catch fish when the moon is on one of its closer approaches as to when it is more distant.

Hypothesis 2: *The moon's light levels affect the fishing.*

Results: 17% of all fish were caught during full moon periods and 14% of all fish were caught during new moon periods. If light played a real role in catch rates we would expect one light condition (bright or dark) to have dominated. Much like our findings with gravity, given the sample size of several thousand data points, catch rates did not change in statistically meaningful ways during new and full moons. Here again, we reject the hypothesis and can safely say changes in light levels from new or full moons have no discernible impact on catch rates. **You'll catch about as many fish under a new moon as you will a full moon all other things laid equal.**

Hypothesis 3: *Moonrise and Moonset improve fishing.*

Results: The average catch rate at moonrise and moonset during any given moon phase is about 20%. This means that on any given day about 20% of the fish in the dataset were caught within 1 hour of moonrise or moonset. Catch rates peaked at the full moon and new moons at roughly 25-28% respectively. Remember full and new moons are closely correlated to sunrise and sunset, which are known peak fishing periods due to lower light levels that give predator fish an advantage over their prey. When we remove the variable of sunrise and sunset by looking and moonrises and moonsets that occur near the middle of the day, we see catch rates near these periods drop off dramatically, bottoming out at 13% which roughly mirrors catch rates for any randomly selected daylight hour. This indicates that **moonrise and moonset as independent variables offer no predictive value for improved fishing.**

In Doug Hannon's 1986 publican "Big Bass Magic," the bass professor himself argues for a strong connection between lunar phases and fishing success. Hannon bolstered this claim by creating a graph of world record catches that occurred between 1970 and 1979 as compared to moon phases. In Hannon's study there appeared to be some correlation between moon phase and world record catches as more catches seemed to take place on or around the new and full moon. He claimed that 73% of catches occurred on three days of either side of the full or new moon, plus the day of each half-moon. While initially this seems impressive, it's important to note that as defined, Hannon has included more than half of all the days in a lunar month! In the figure below, I have updated Hannon's graph to include new World Record catches that have been confirmed since the original publishing date of Hannon's book. As defined previously by Hannon, peak lunar days which

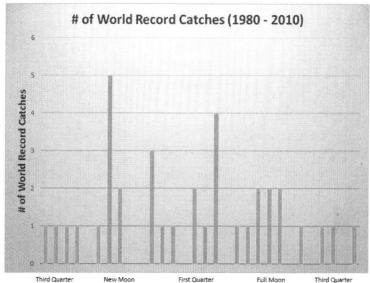

comprise 51% of a lunar month now only yield 55% of the catches as compared to the 73% Hannon noted. The full moon bias has vanished and there isn't a strong correlation with catch rates and any particular moon phase. This is compelling evidence to further bolster the case that lunar periods have little if anything to do with the feeding cycles of fish.

Conclusion

What does all this mean? In my opinion, the facts and data paint an incredibly clear picture. We've shown that gravity, reflected light levels, and moonset and moonrise, do not have statistically verifiable impacts on catch rates. The pervasive myth in fishing to the contrary is a prime example of an illusory correlation. **Fishermen wrongly assigning meaning to moonrise and moonset (especially during full and new moons) when the only truly impactful variable is the lower light levels due to sunrise and sunset that happen to coincide with these time periods.**

Here's a sample exchange: Angler, "I don't care what your statistics say. Last July around sunset I notice the moon was rising and I immediately sped to my best spot on the lake and threw my best bait! Wouldn't you know it I boated a huge bass! Clearly it was because of the moonrise." My Response: "No, you were fishing the best spot on the lake with a proven bait during a low light period. That's why you caught the fish. The moon had nothing to do with it!"

I'd love for a connection to be there. A predictable and rhythmic way to increase catch rates? Sign me up! Beyond the fact that it's just not in the data, I see no mechanism via which fish would be influenced by the moon in a lake. Gravitational pull is too weak. Light levels don't seem to matter. Are we to assume fish sit there like gators, lurking just beneath the surface, watching for a moon event to signal them to start feeding? What do they do when it's cloudy? As much as I'd like the moon myth to be true the data just says it is not.

I doubt this study will change many minds on the matter of the moon. Superstitions are incredibly hard to disprove and many will choose to hang on to comforting myths, even if the data shows them to be just that. Am I saying that if I was on a lake by myself and noticed the moon coming up that I wouldn't jump to my best spot? No, I suspect I would. In the words of Duck Dynasty's Si Robertson, "Hey Jack, you never know."

However, I certainly wouldn't lose any sleep if I had a fishing trip planned that didn't coincide with a moon phase.

HP Tip: Don't ignore moon phases. Particularly in the world of musky fishing, plan your trips around them, especially new and full moons. Minimize fishing pressure and maximize your chances by making sure you arrive a few days before the masses do!

When to Fish

"It has always been my private conviction that any man who pits his intelligence against a fish and loses has it coming"
– John Steinbeck

Time of Day

Data from tens of thousands of catches was compiled to create the graph on the following page. Each color represents the percentage of catches that occurred during that time slot during a given month. For example, 7% of all fish caught in the month of April were caught between the hours of 9am-10am. Data for twilight periods was either unavailable or had a sample size too small to be of statistical significance. In the interest of transparency, there is a possible "effort bias" in the data that should be discussed. More specifically the data tells us the number of fish caught in a given hour long period, but it does not tell us how many hours fishermen spent fishing that period. Therefore, it is possible if not likely that some periods show depressed catch rates simply because fewer fishermen fished during those periods. As an example, throughout the year, the data indicates that more fish were caught on a consistent basis in evenings as opposed to mornings. I suspect that what is innate here isn't a fish's preference for feeding in the evening but a human preference for sleeping in. I do not believe that this potential bias renders the data useless, but I do believe anglers should be mindful of it as they consider the implications and develop their own fishing strategies throughout the year. Possible bias aside, there are several key takeaways that should immediately jump out to High Percentage Fishermen. First, in the spring, peak feeding periods occur during the warmest parts of the day. Afternoon catch rates significantly outperform the first half of the day. Next, we see that once the season progresses past post-spawn, the middle of the day tends to fish poorly with catch rates running as low as 30% of what could be achieved during low light periods. Finally, there is bad news for tournament anglers, most tournaments are held from 7am-3pm which misses much of the peak fishing periods each day!

Peak Fishing Times by Month

Time	*Jan	*Feb	March	April	May	June	July	Aug	Sep	Oct	Nov	*Dec
6 am			0%	2%	3%	3%	4%	3%	2%	0%	0%	
7 am			2%	5%	6%	4%	5%	6%	5%	2%	1%	
8 am			4%	6%	7%	5%	6%	7%	4%	4%	3%	
9 am			6%	7%	8%	6%	7%	7%	6%	6%	6%	
10 am			10%	8%	10%	7%	5%	6%	8%	10%	11%	
11 am			12%	8%	9%	6%	5%	6%	8%	12%	13%	
12 pm			4%	3%	4%	2%	2%	2%	3%	4%	6%	
1 pm			9%	6%	7%	5%	4%	4%	6%	9%	13%	
2 pm			11%	6%	7%	6%	4%	5%	6%	11%	15%	
3 pm			11%	6%	6%	5%	4%	4%	6%	11%	14%	
4 pm			10%	6%	6%	4%	4%	4%	6%	10%	12%	
5 pm			10%	7%	5%	5%	5%	4%	7%	10%	4%	
6 pm			8%	9%	5%	8%	7%	7%	9%	8%	1%	
7 pm			3%	11%	7%	11%	10%	11%	11%	3%	0%	
8 pm			1%	6%	5%	11%	13%	12%	6%	1%	0%	
9 pm			0%	2%	2%	3%	9%	6%	2%	0%	0%	

*Figures unavailable, shaded using estimates

0-1.5%	Poor
1.5-5.0%	Fair
5.1-7.0%	Good
7.0-9.0%	Better
9.0%+	Peak

HP Tip: If you hire a guide to learn a new body of water, make sure you talk with the guide ahead of time to ensure you'll be on the water during peak times of the day.

Time of Week

In considering which day of the week to fish, busy schedules often make the decision for us through a simple process of elimination. Intuitively this choice may not seem all that impactful, but in truth, the data paints an entirely different picture. In reviewing which day of the week had the most impact on fishing success, catch rates were compared to overall fishing pressure on a given day of the week. I collected fishing pressure data by calling several parks departments who staffed entry booths to collect launch fees on lakes which were used almost exclusively for fishing. With this simple request, I was provided data on the average number of boats launched on each day of the week. It will come as no surprise that weekends received far greater pressure than your average weekday. Once I had this data the method of comparing catch rates in relative terms of fishing pressure was straightforward. If a Saturday saw 25% of the total launches in a week, we would expect 25% of the total fish caught in the week to occur on Saturdays. Saturday catch rate percentages above or below this number would indicate a positive or negative impact in relative terms. In this way, I compared the day per week catch distribution of tens of thousands of catches to the average fishing pressure a body of water received on a given day of the week. The graph on the following page illustrates the findings:

Catch Rate

Best

Better

Worst

| | Sunday | Monday | Tuesday | Wednesday | Thursday | Friday | Saturday |

3X

2X

Baseline

86

The previous graph is amongst the most significant of all the observations I made from reviewing the data set. On average, weekends receive many times the fishing pressure as weekday, yet the average weekday produces a disproportionately larger number of the total fish caught in a given week. On a per hour basis, a Wednesday delivers more than 3 times the number of fish as a Saturday. One of the most impactful choices a High Percentage Fisherman can make is picking the day of the week to fish. Of course it isn't really about the day of the week, it is fundamentally about minimizing competitive pressure from other anglers. **As it pertains to catch rates, in the statistical sense, fishing pressure matters far more than all but the most extreme weather phenomena. I'd much rather fish an east wind Wednesday than a west wind Saturday.**

HP Tip: If you must fish weekends, you will likely need to use other approaches to minimize pressure such as fishing remote bodies of water, fishing deeper, or fishing at night.

Time of Year

"Anyone can be a fisherman in March."
— Ernest Hemmingway

To be fair to Mr. Hemmingway I've changed his original quote from May to March. Although if you are reading this in Wisconsin, May would be more fitting. The point though is the same in both cases, fishing pre-spawn and spawn periods is widely accepted by many anglers to be the best time of the year to get a shot at the fish of a lifetime. There is a common misconception that bass weigh the most in the spring because of the eggs they carry. This can certainly be true for smaller fish, but it may not be true for larger fish. A 4-pound bass will hold roughly the same number of eggs as a 14-pound bass. As a result, the eggs make up a larger portion of the overall mass in smaller fish as compared to the larger fish. Larger fish on the other hand, often weigh more in the summer period when they are at their peak feeding levels. For them, regularly available food adds more total mass than a comparatively small percentage of weight they gain from carrying eggs.

The data below is taken from the Texas ShareLunker Program. The program encourages anglers to turn over 13-pound plus fish from October 1st through April 30th in an effort to spawn the fish in captivity to create genetically superior fry

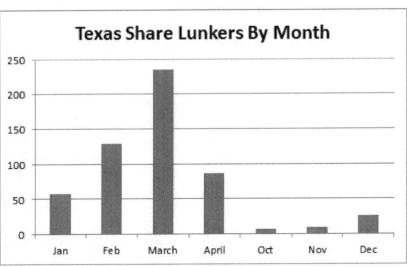

for stocking. The fish are typically kept for one spawn cycle and then returned to their home waters. The success of the program is widely debated in Texas as many of the lunker bass die despite intense efforts to care for the fish. The data is very clear that far more lunker fish are taken in the spring than in the fall. Undoubtedly this is because the spring is the one time of year when virtually all big fish, regardless of their preferred layer venture into shallow water layer where they are more susceptible to angling. Whether or not the program is ultimately deemed a success may still be up for debate, but the program has yielded detailed catch information spanning nearly 30 years on over 500 bass weighing more than 13 pounds caught in the state. Amongst other things, this information includes date, location, and a description of the lures that the fish were caught on. Nearly 45% of the ShareLunker bass caught over the years have been caught on Lake Fork. Fork is considered by many to be the bass fishing Mecca of the world. Famous for big numbers of large fish, the lake has routinely coughed up a huge percentage of the total ShareLunkers caught annually. Greenwich Mean Time serves as the time standard for much of the world. Similarly, I frequently use the term, "Fork Standard Time" as a way in which to develop a time standard by which we may determine peak periods on distant bodies of water. The ShareLunker data indicates by far the best month for big fish is March. Peak periods within the month of March vary year to year based on local weather patterns which influence water temperature and thus the spawn. Generally speaking though, the second and third weeks of March produce the most big fish.

HP Tip: In the spring the sun advances north roughly 500 miles per month. Knowing this, you can determine the likely peak period at your home lake by estimating the difference North or South you are from Lake Fork and offsetting by the appropriate time. For instance, Chicago is roughly 800 miles North of Lake Fork, and thus, the peak period in that region is likely to occur in mid to late May (6-7 weeks after Lake Fork).

Where to Fish

"The only thing bigger than a fish without a picture is a fish that was almost caught." - Unknown

A major part of successful High Percentage Fishing is first choosing where to fish. As fundamental as it sounds, this is a basic step that many anglers spend far too little time considering. For some the choice of where to fish is rigid in the sense that they lack mobility or variety in local bodies of water. For most, however, the lakes they regularly fish are often more a function of convenience than conscious decision making. As with all aspects of High Percentage Fishing, the key is purposeful data based decision making. In this section, we will explore a few of the tactics you can use to drastically improve your catch rates with a little bit of upfront homework.

Which Regions

This book is written to serve as a guide to help folks catch more fish regardless of size. However, if anglers are after trophy class fish, the topic of regional differences across the country cannot be avoided. Though far from authoritative, this section will share a few comments that might guide High Percentage Fishermen in the direction of larger fish.

Numbers of fish can be had throughout much of the lower 48. However, if you are chasing fish over 10lbs, there are few things more important than the region of the country you focus your fishing efforts on. Simply put, much of the country is too cold and has too short a growing season to generate significant numbers of large fish. Virtually any southern state, however, has the potential to produce large fish and most do every year. In this case as before, we are talking percentages, so in terms of statistics which states produce your best shot a trophy class largemouth bass? Broadly speaking, in the US, there are three major regions which produce the majority of fish caught each year in excess of 10lbs; Florida, Texas, and California. A quick look at the top 25 largemouth bass ever caught and weighed reveals California (Murphy territory) as the dominate state. In fact, 19 out of the top 25 fish come from California most notably Castaic Lake, CA (6 of top 25), Miramar Reservoir, CA (5 of top 25), and Lake Dixon, CA (3 of the top 25). Interestingly, the tiny trout stocked Lake Dixon, with only 76 surface acres has produced the largest bass on record. The fish nicknamed "Dottie," at one point had a verified weight of over 25lbs; more than 10% larger than any other largemouth bass ever caught. However, this fish was inadvertently foul hooked and as such is not a recognizable World Record. Currently, two fish are tied for the World Record, one bass weighing 22.3lbs caught in Lake Biwa in Japan in 2009 and George Perry's fish caught in Montgomery Lake, GA in 1932. Interestingly, no authenticated photographic evidence, physical evidence, or independent confirmation of weight exists for Perry's fish. If extraordinary claims require extraordinary evidence, in this case, we are left grossly wanting. In the eyes of many anglers, including my own, it makes Perry's record highly suspect. Outside of California, Florida has only one fish in the top 25 and Texas completely blanks missing the list altogether. Certainly, in terms of World Record class fish, California has perhaps the best overall odds of producing such a fish. However, if you broaden the scope of trophy fish to include numbers of 10lb plus fish, the waters become murky (pun intended). Using broad strokes, let's consider a few pros and cons for each of the major giant producing regions. The rest I'll leave up to you!

California:

Pros:
-More top 50 fish than any other state.
-Verified fish over 25lbs (Dottie)
-Stable warm weather that allows long growing seasons with little risk for extreme heat to cause metabolic burnout.
-Water temperatures cool enough to sustain stocked trout populations, a common denominator in many of the state's biggest fish producing reservoirs.

Cons:
-Perhaps the most pressured bodies of water in the country.
-Comparatively few bodies of water.
-Many of the biggest fish (including most of Murphy's fish) seem to have a preference for the deep water lake layer.

Florida:

Pros:
-A huge number of natural lakes.
-Many lakes with springs which help moderate water temperatures.
- The northern half of the state is cool enough to avoid metabolic burnout.
-Generally shallow bodies of water that can be easily fished with live bait.
-Florida-strain fish with genetic growth rate and maximum size attainment advantage.

Cons:
-Southern lakes may be too warm to produce record class fish.
-Many bodies of water do not lend themselves well to fishing with artificial lures.
-Florida-strain bass are less susceptible to artificial lures.

Texas:

<u>Pros:</u>
-Several large reservoirs with a history of producing hundreds of trophy class fish annually.
-Most of the state's major reservoirs are far enough north to avoid metabolic burnout.
-Large numbers of trophy class fish taken from the mid lake layer.

<u>Cons:</u>
-Considerable fishing pressure on many lakes, particularly in the spring.
-Many of the reservoirs are so vast that adequately learning them can be a difficult and time-consuming task.
-A mix of Florida and Northern strain bass which may create genetic headwinds achieving maximum size potential.
-Northern lakes have a shorter growing season than California or Florida.
-Vast distances between many lakes. (It's true, everything is bigger in Texas.)

Selecting Local Bodies of Water

One of the most important decisions High Percentage Fishermen can make is selecting the local body of water they are going to fish. Too often anglers select lakes based on convenience, but convenience does not put fish in the boat. The concept of High Percentage Fishing is about using data to make better decisions. There is a huge amount of data available that can help fishermen figure out which lakes in their region have the best chances of producing numbers of quality fish.

One of the best resources out there are regional fishing forums. To name just a few, in Texas, there is-www.texasfishingforum.com, in California www.lmhooked.com, and in the Midwest www.lakelink.com. Virtually every state or region has similar sites where like-minded anglers get together and share information and best practices about fishing in their areas. These sites frequently contain a wealth of information that might otherwise take years to learn. Fishermen, in general, can be secretive, and the sites are not likely to provide you with GPS coordinates of the best spots out there, but the vast majority of participants on these sites are good natured folks who love talking about their passion. I'd highly encourage High Percentage Fishermen to mine these sites for information pertaining to the best local waters and tactics. You'll quickly learn which local waters are regularly producing fish and which lakes might be going through a tough cycle. You may even be able to ask questions directly about which waters are best and get answers tailored to the particular type of fish you are seeking (trophy, quality, numbers.) It is also a great way to meet potential fishing partners or mentors. If you are able to find a great fishing mentor they may be more than happy to take you out. Some may share in a few hours' tips and tricks that that took them a lifetime to acquire. Now that is a high percentage method!

In selecting a body of water, one of the most important considerations should be the amount of pressure the lake gets. The more fishing and boating pressure, the higher the odds the lake is going to fish tough. Often pressure is a direct function of population density. The closer the proximity to large numbers of people the higher the probability the lake is going to get a lot of pressure. Google Maps can be a great tool to use to help identify isolated bodies of water that may be off the beaten path that are worthy of additional research. Truly secret lakes probably no longer exist, but it is certainly possible to find low-pressure gems that can yield catch rates far above normal levels for the area. I also use Google Maps to gauge the percentage of shoreline that has been built up for homes and to judge the size and number of boat launches. Obviously, fewer homes generally means lower pressure, and boat launches with few parking spaces can lower pressure by reducing accessibility.

Fishing maps or internet sources may also contain stocking and electric shock studies conducted by the DNR that can also be useful in helping to identify high potential bodies of water. I was once on a weeklong walleye fishing trip on a large chain of lakes in Northern Wisconsin. After several days of unsuccessful fishing, I was able to use stocking and shock data to determine which lakes on the chain likely had the highest concentration of walleye. This observation helped turn the trip around with several days of great fishing! By narrowing down my focus from 20+ lakes to two lakes, I was able to find fish and identify a productive pattern. More importantly, I was able to fish with confidence knowing I was fishing smarter!

HP Tip: Google Earth (different from Google Maps) has a function that allows you to see historic imagery. This can be a fantastic tool if you are fishing lakes that have had significant water fluctuations in the past. By looking at years gone by you may be able to identify structure and cover on lakes during low water periods that are now submerged in a higher water period.

Selecting Where in the Lake to Fish

The first place to begin when trying to determine where to fish on a given lake is a good topographical map. They are indispensable in effectively managing time on the water. A little bit of time spent studying a map prior to a trip can save you hours of search time and dramatically increase catch rates. Before we can have a meaningful discussion on how to dissect a lake and locate high probability fishing locations, it is important to spend a little time on some basic terminology.

Buck Perry was one of the first fishermen to use the word "structure" in the 1950's. Over the years, the term has evolved repeatedly to mean different things to different anglers. Similarly, the term "cover" has changed somewhat over time. For the purposes of this discussion, structure should be considered any inorganic item that is a natural part of the lake bottom. This could include points, humps, creek channels, rocks, flats, funnel points, multi-directional drop offs, and ledges. Cover, on the other hand, is any item that has been added to the lake or is organic in origin. This would include things like weeds, trees, stumps, docks, brush piles, and manmade fish attractors. As a general rule of thumb the more types of structure and cover you can find in one location the higher the probability the area will hold fish. John Hope suggested looking for two types of structure and two types of cover. Hope and Perry agreed that structure was the most important factors of the two. Perry once said, "You can find structure without fish, but you cannot find fish without structure." Most forms of structure are generally visible on topographical maps; however certain types of cover may change frequently enough that it is not identified on maps. Nonetheless, fishermen can use this strategy to key in high probability locations that are prime candidates for further investigation once on the water. An example of two types of cover adjacent to two types of structure is shown in the figure below:

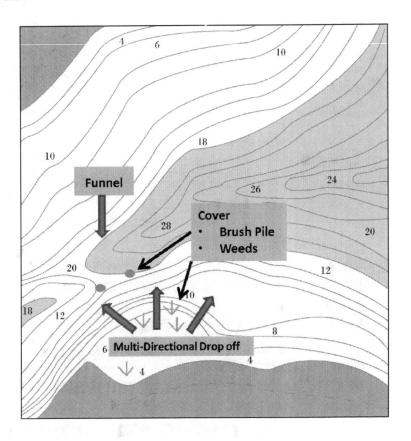

Seasonal Considerations

Daily and seasonal routines are followed by virtually every living creature on this planet. Bass are no different. They have biological needs that must be met, and the fish develop habits that over time have helped them achieve this goal. This point became particularly well engrained in my brain when I looked at years worth of my own catch data on a couple of lakes. I laid out a map and color coded each catch based on the season the catch had occurred in. What became immediately apparent is that seasonal movements followed an easily identifiable pattern of shallow and deep water movements. Almost as if the lake as a whole inhaled in the spring and fall drawing fish shallow and exhaled in the summer and winter driving them deeper. As John Hope's studies made clear, most fish do not have massive home ranges. Large fish over 7lbs may have home ranges that are rarely larger than perhaps quarter mile in diameter. Smaller fish may have ranges that can be several times this size, but typically fish don't just randomly swim around a lake. They stick with what is close, they stick with what they know, they stick with what has worked. It's useful to keep this important point in mind when we talk about the seasonal movement of bass. It's true bass move with the season, but remember most fish are not moving all that far. They are simply shifting within their already defined home range and preferred depth layer. A deep water fish that spends the majority of its time on offshore structure in the main lake is not likely to be found in 3 feet of water in the back of a 6-mile creek arm chasing shad in the fall. They simply don't move that far. Fish caught in the backs of creek arms are likely shallow or mid-layer residents of that arm year round.

Pre-Spawn

The exact start of pre-spawn behavior in largemouth bass varies by year. In general, we can say pre-spawn behavior is well underway when water temps hit 55 degrees in most bodies of water. However, I have personally observed fish staging outside of spawning flats in temperatures as low as the mid to upper 40s. In all cases, the behavior is the same. Bass will begin feeding more aggressively as their metabolic rate increases in the warming water and they will begin moving from the deeper portions of their preferred layer to shallower extents nearer to historic spawning flats. Very often bass will use underwater creek channels to make this migration. Creek bends in the 8-14 foot range can be great areas to target as well as main lake points between winter holding areas and spawning grounds.

HP Tip: Jigs and soft plastic worms are the largest producers of fish during this period.

Spawn

60 degrees is generally accepted to be the start of the preferred spawning temperature of largemouth bass, however, I have seen fish on beds in water as cold as 55 degrees. Much of the overall progression of the spawn depends on the prevailing weather patterns that happen to be occurring that year. Warm trends followed by cold snaps can push fish back off beds and there may be several starts and stops to the spawning cycle.

Males kick off the spawn by fanning out roundish beds on the lake bottom 1-3 feet in diameter. Typically these beds are in hard bottom flats located in 1-3 feet of water. Deeper beds out to perhaps 8 feet or beyond are not uncommon particularly on highly pressured lakes. Females staged nearby will then select a bed and male. There is a common misconception that only males guard the nest once the female has laid her eggs. As any fisherman who has caught a fish larger than 7lbs off a bed can tell you, this is demonstrably false. However the egg guarding duties are split, large females very often participate in the process making the spawn the highest percentage time of the year for the average angler to land a trophy.

Spawning bass rarely feed, they've got more important things on their minds. Therefore, fish that are caught off beds are generally caught when the bass hits a lure it perceives as a threat to its eggs or when it has used its mouth to move a lure off the bed as an act of simple housekeeping. This creates an ethical dilemma for many anglers who view it as less sporting and potentially damaging to future bass populations. I feel these concerns are very valid and should be taken seriously by all bass anglers.

Below I have included some tips to help catch spawning bass. I ask that all anglers practice catch and release during the spawn. Quite literally the future of our sport depends on it!

Tips for Catching Spawning Fish

The first step in catching bedded fish is to determine the mood of the fish. Skilled trophy hunters during this time of the year have become highly tuned to the reactions of bedded bass when lures are presented. Skittish fish that immediately flee the bed are not "locked" and could be difficult or impossible to catch. Additionally, fish bedding in more visible areas may receive immense pressure from anglers. After being caught multiple times out of simple necessity for self-preservation, these fish may be incredibly difficult to coax into biting. As a general strategy for High Percentage Fishing, these bass are better off left alone. Mark them in your GPS and check them another time, but for now, keep moving and try to locate fish that hold tightly to their beds. Once you've located a bass that is locked on its bed, begin by throwing a brightly colored bait that is easily visible in the water. Not being able to see your bait is a bigger concern than using the wrong color. Cast well past the bed, and crawl the bait to the center of the bed. Use your rod tip to impart action to the lure and note the reaction of the bass. If you are able to generate aggressive behavior out of the fish, immediately cast back and keep casting back until the fish bites. If you are still unable to get a reaction out of the bass, switch baits. I've found plastic lizards, various creature baits, tubes, bluegill, or bullhead imitators to be prolific producers. Similarly, change size, up or down as necessary. Don't be afraid to throw the biggest bait you have in your box if you need to. If a large fish is particularly skittish it may be wise to place a marker buoy just off of the bed. This will allow you to rest the bed for a period and then return and make long precise casts from a distance great enough to minimize the chances of spooking the fish.

HP Tip: Many trophy class fishermen spend a lot of time on the water during the spawn, but spend very little time actually fishing. They cruise the shallows marking the locations of the biggest bass. Given that big bass have small home ranges, they know these fish will be close by during other times of the year.

Summer

On lakes where shad is the dominate forage, much of the summertime feeding behavior of bass will be driven by the movement of shad. In the summertime, shad are typically found in open water during the day feeding on algae. In bright light shad have a visual advantage over bass and can freely feed on an abundance of open water algae that forms in the warm portions of the main lake. As light levels drop, the visual advantage shifts to predators and shad often make a daily migration to nearby shallow water to shelter down during low light periods. This makes the shallow water bite in the summer particularly good at dusk and dawn. It is typically best to target shallow water that is close to the main lake. Shad are unlikely to make long daily movements to the back of creek arms in the summer. It's simply more movement than is necessary. Once the sun comes up shad move back out into open water to feed on algae. Before your trip, spend time reviewing a topographical map. On a new body of water in any of the warm water seasons, I recommend eliminating water over 25 feet deep. Water this deep is difficult to fish efficiently and is usually only practical when you are extremely confident bass are present in the location. This level of certainty is difficult to achieve on new bodies of water. Additionally, in the summer thermoclines very often develop around this level which creates environments too oxygen-poor to support much fish life at greater depths. Next with the exception of springtime or lakes with very little fishing pressure, I would also eliminate areas that are more than 100 yards from at least 8 feet of water. Shallow areas get immense pressure by other fishermen, are more susceptible to temperature changes due to cold fronts, and may suffer from oxygen depletion in the summer. Certainly there can be fish present in shallow water, but statistically speaking I believe High Percentage Fishermen are better off leaving this water for the masses for much of the season. With the remaining water, which may be as little as 20% of the lake, focus on searching for funnel points, multi-directional drop offs, and offshore flats, adjacent to multiple types of cover. I find the less common a type of cover is in a particular body of water, the higher the probability it will hold fish if it is adjacent to structure. Intermittent cover tends to hold bigger fish in more predictable locations than massive thick weed beds that stretch on for acres. As an example, patches of grass near the shallow end of a funnel point in a lake with very little grass is far more likely to hold fish than a run of the mill grass flat in a lake filled with grass. It's a simple case of concentration as a result of scarcity.

Once you arrive at the lake, the next step is to visually check out the areas you marked as likely fish holding locations on your map. One of the first things I do when arriving at a new lake is to use my depth finder to graph a major main lake point in detail. I'll start shallow and work my way out to around the 25-foot mark in an effort to identify the depth most fish seem to be holding at. Ideally, I'm looking for fish activity in 8-12 feet of water as this range provides the best mix of low fishing pressure and ease of fishing. The whole process may take several passes to get a solid idea of which depth most fish are holding at. If I mark a concentration of fish at a particular depth, that's the depth I'll begin to fish at the prime locations I've previously identified on the topographical map. Along the way, I'm also looking for isolated grass patches as they are favored cover for big bass.

HP Tip: Make sure your casts are parallel to the depth you are targeting. If fish are located in 12 feet of water and your boat is sitting in 18 feet of water and you are casting toward shore into 4 feet of water, your lure may only be spending a few seconds in your target depth. Conversely, if you are casting parallel to your target depth, your lure will be spending the majority of each cast in the target zone.

Fall

The fall provides anglers with some of the most predictable fishing of the year. Throughout most of the summer, forage fish such as threadfin shad have spent much of their time roaming offshore portions of lakes freely feeding on an abundance of algae. Much of the freshwater algae common in the US blooms most prolifically in water between 77 and 90 degrees. Warm water and an abundance of nutrients brought to the lake from spring rains can often sustain offshore algae through the entire summer. However, as the first cool nights in fall start to occur, offshore water temperatures begin to fall. Once main lake water temperatures drop below 77 degrees open water algae blooms begin to decline. While this is occurring offshore, shallower portions of creek arms will still be warmed by daytime sunlight and maintain water temperatures sufficient for algae growth. It is at this time that shad will begin their migration from their main lake summertime haunts into the back of creek arms chasing their receding food source. Once the water temps drop to the mid to upper 50s, even though algae may still be present, the shad will reverse their migration and head back to open water. Below 55 degrees, rapid temperature changes common in the shallows can kill shad. Deeper open water tends to moderate temperature swings and reduces this risk. When fishing in the fall, my first approach is to check the main lake water temperature. This will give me an idea of how long the shad migration has likely been in progress. Water temperatures in the 70s offer an indication that the migration has only recently begun and I will concentrate my search on the first 1/3 of creek arms closest to the main body. Similarly, water in the low 60s or high 50s would indicate the shad are as far back into the creeks as they are likely to go. Once my search area is identified I'll use electronics to search creek arms extensively before I begin fishing. When bait balls are located the task then becomes picking baits that are best able to present at the depth bass are attacking the shad at. Again, this will change from hour to hour and you'll need to rely heavily on your electronics for this information. I spend very little time fishing areas in the fall where shad are not present.

Winter

Winter can be one of the hardest times to target bass. Metabolic rates are at yearly lows, and many fish may go as long as five days between feedings. Winter locations tend to closely match offshore summer locations. Frequently they are main lake spots that offer enough deep water to moderate temperatures while still meeting the basic biological needs of bass. Check main lake points and creek channels adjacent to deep water structure out to 40 feet.

HP Tip: It may seem counterintuitive, but locations marked as prime spots on many commercially available maps very often turn out to be great fishing spots; particularly if you are fishing low-pressure periods. These maps are products, and the creators generally spend a fair amount of time speaking with local experts or bait shop owners who have a vested interest in seeing anglers succeed.

What to Fish With

*"Fishing is much more than fish. It is the great occasion when
we may return to the fine simplicity of our forefathers."*
— Herbert Hoover

Lures

The Texas ShareLunker data provides an excellent source of data on trophy bass fishing with more than 500 data points spanning several decades on fish over 13lbs caught between October 1st and April 30th. As High Percentage Fishermen, analyzing the data can help shed light on which lures and techniques are most effective during which season. There are certainly some limitations to the conclusions we can draw from the data as all fish in the sample set were caught in the state of Texas. However, much of the data closely aligns with key points made by Hannon, Hope, and Murphy, suggesting usefulness outside of southern reservoirs. We've already established the peak fishing months from the ShareLunker data and explained how to determine the peak in your area based on the latitude of your home waters. As High Percentage Fishermen the next question becomes, "so what are they catching them on?" The answer can be seen in the first figure on the following page. **Soft plastic baits account for nearly 75% of all ShareLunkers caught**. Hannon and Murphy suggested this would be the case decades ago, noting that soft plastic baits seem to be one of the few lures bass do not seem to develop learned negative associations with over time. This notion is solidly reinforced by the data when we separate the success rate of soft baits vs. hard baits over time. The second figure on the following page shows that **the percentage of ShareLunkers caught on soft plastic baits has nearly doubled over the past 25 years while the percentage caught on hard baits has fallen roughly 20%**. Soft plastic baits are mostly noiseless by nature, move naturally in the water, and have a texture, not unlike many naturally occurring prey species. All these factors combine to make soft plastic baits difficult lures for fish to become accustomed to

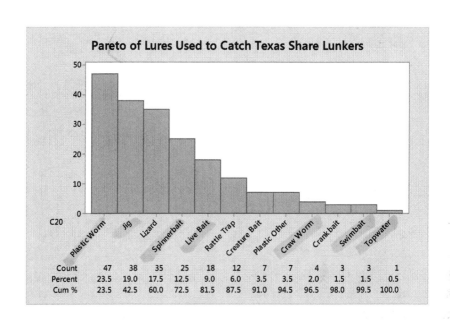

Pareto of Lures Used to Catch Texas Share Lunkers

	Plastic Worm	Jig	Lizard	Spinnerbait	Live Bait	Rattle Trap	Creature Bait	Plastic Other	Craw Worm	Crankbait	Swimbait	Topwater
Count	47	38	35	25	18	12	7	7	4	3	3	1
Percent	23.5	19.0	17.5	12.5	9.0	6.0	3.5	3.5	2.0	1.5	1.5	0.5
Cum %	23.5	42.5	60.0	72.5	81.5	87.5	91.0	94.5	96.5	98.0	99.5	100.0

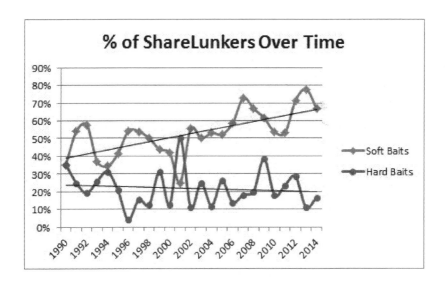

% of ShareLunkers Over Time

over time. Many hard baits, on the other hand, create noise and vibration that fish can learn over time and develop negative associations with. To be clear, there are still many large fish caught on hard baits, but in terms of High Percentage Fishing, a springtime angler on the hunt for a trophy is well advised to throw plastic.

Expanding on the big bass preference for plastic, I've further stratified the ShareLunker data highlighting which lures were most effective in producing trophies in which month. Again, adjustments should be made based on your North/South distance from Lake Fork in Texas.

Lure Effectiveness			
Month	1st	2nd	3rd
Jan	Jig	Worm	Crankbait
Feb	Jig	Worm	Spinnerbait
March	Worm	Jig	Lizard
April	Worm	Lizard	Jig
July	Worm	Lizard	Jig
August	Worm	Lizard	Jig
Sep	Worm	Spinnerbait	Lizard
Oct	Worm	Crankbait	Spinnerbait
Nov	Jig	Crankbait	Worm
Dec	Crankbait	Jig	Spinnerbait

HP Tip: The data only shows us the number of trophy fish that have actually been boated. Soft plastic baits tend to have one hook, which have far higher landing percentages than the treble hooks on many hard types of bait. If you are not trophy fishing, hard baits may provide more action during the pre-spawn as they cover more water in search of active fish.

Color

In terms of color, the data paints a very clear picture. Across the entire data set (thousands of data points) variants of black, particularly black and blue for big bass, account for more than 30% of all catches, more than twice that of any other color. Black creates a dark silhouette that makes lures more visible in the water and also serves to provide contrast on the actual bait making it more difficult for fish to key in on unnatural components of the lure. **When in doubt throw black!** Watermelon, Pumpkinseed, and natural colors (matching local forage) were runners-up.

HP Tip: Black lures are even more effective in low light conditions. Consider using lighter colored baits in clear water or during the brightest parts of the day.

Line

The chart on the following page is meant to serve as a basic guideline for High Percentage Fishermen when selecting which line to use for a particular type of bait. Smaller diameter line is stealthy line. It improves lure action and ultimately generates more strikes. Naturally there is a balance to be struck between line diameter and strength. Line technology has improved by leaps and bounds over the past decade and break-offs can now be rare events with proper line selection. I've developed this chart through years of personal experience but created it by assuming average fish on average lakes across the country. If bass on a particular lake run on the smaller size, High Percentage Fishermen would be wise to select line on the lower end of the range.

Line Selector (Lb Test)			
Lure	Mono	Fluoro	Braid
Wacky Rig		4-8 lbs	
Drop Shot		6-8 lbs	
Shaky Head		8-12 lbs	
Carolina Rig		15-20 lbs	
Buzzbaits	15-20 lbs		30-50 lbs
Frogs			40-65 lbs
Hard Bodied Topwaters	12-20 lbs		30-50 lbs
Jerkbaits		8-12 lbs	
Lipless Cranks	8-14 lbs		
Shallow Cranks (1-4 feet)		12-17 lbs	
Medium Cranks (4-12 feet)		10-15 lbs	
Deep Cranks (12+ feet)		10-15 lbs	
Flipping Jigs		15-20 lbs	30-60 lbs
Football Jigs		12-17 lbs	
Swimming Jigs		15-20 lbs	
Chatterbaits	12-17 lbs	12-17 lbs	
Spinnerbaits	12-17 lbs	12-17 lbs	
Soft Plastic Worms	8-15 lbs	8-15 lbs	20-30 lbs
Small Plastic Swim Bait		10-15 lbs	
Large Plastic Swim Bait		15-20 lbs	
Small Hard Swimbait		15-20	
Large Hard Swimbait		17-25	30-60 lbs

HP Tip: Line size has virtually no impact on strike rates at night. Don't be afraid to bulk up to avoid losing fish!

The Bass Equation

"There's a fine line between fishing and just standing on the shore like an idiot." - Steven Wright

The "Bass Equation" is a probabilistic model I developed to estimate the number of bass likely to be caught on a given body of water based on several key variables. The model is based on a similar model called the "Drake Equation" popularized by Frank Drake in 1961 which attempted to model the likely number of advanced civilizations in the galaxy. The Bass Equation works by asking anglers to estimate the value for several key variables that influence catch rates. Working through the process can be an enlightening exercise that can help anglers better develop a plan of attack for a particular lake. The figure on the next page works through an example calculation based on a hypothetical Lake X.

Step 1

Total Acreage: This calculation is very straightforward; simply input the total acreage of the lake. This can often be found on the internet, most topographic maps, or local bait shops.

Step 2

Acreage Holding Fish: This calculation determines what portion of the lake is likely to hold bass. A good rule of thumb is that in the vast majority of lakes, 20% of the lake is going to hold 80% of the bass. For much of the year, vast portions of water below the thermocline can be ruled out simply for physiological reasons; deep water simply does not hold enough oxygen to support bass in warm weather. Furthermore, most anglers become inefficient at depths much beyond 20 feet. For many of the lakes in the country, this will eliminate large portions of water. Suggested range of inputs: 10%-40%.

Step	Variable to Estimate	Lake X	
		Calc.	Example Calc.
1	What is the total Acerage?	1200	Total Acreage
2	Total Acres in Lake that Support Bass	240	Step 1 * .2
3	Catchable bass	2400	Step 2 * 10
4	Bass Eating on a Given Day	1200	Step 3 / 2
5	Bass That Will Strike Your Lure	120	Step 4 * .1
6	Catchable Fish in area you fish	4	Step 5 * ((Acres fished/hr)/(Acres that support bass)
7	Fisherman's Bonus	5.2	Step 6 * 1.3
8	Fishing Pressure Factor	2.6	Step 7 / 2
9	Land Percentage	1.95	Step 8 * .75
	Result: (Est. Fish/Hr)	1.95	

Step 3

Catchable Bass: This step determines how many bass are likely to be in the fishable acreage of the lake. On average, a healthy lake will hold around 10 bass per acre. Unhealthy lakes might have populations much lower, and extraordinarily fertile lakes might have bass populations that approach twice this level or more for short periods of time. Suggested range of inputs: 1-20

Step 4

Hungry Bass: This step estimates the number of bass that are likely to feed on a particular day. In the summer bass can digest a full stomach as fast as 2-3 days. In the wintertime, it can take five or more days. As a result in the best case scenario of summer probably only half the bass will need to feed on a given day. You can determine the percentage likely to be feeding by creating the fraction (1/(days to digest)). In the summer this number will likely be 50%; in the winter, it will likely be approximately 20%. Suggested range of inputs: 0.2 - 0.5.

Step 5

Bass That Will Strike Your Lure: This step attempts to estimate the number of bass that have seen your bait and will strike the lure becoming hooked. This is a potentially daunting variable but fortunately, the Bass Professor Doug Hannon has provided us with an estimate of this number. Hannon tags this percentage at roughly 1 in 10. My own personal belief is that the 10% number is a good estimate for moving hard baits such as crank or spinnerbaits. I believe this percentage likely increases for slower moving plastic baits. The reality is it is much easier to fool a bass with a plastic worm than it is with a crankbait. I estimate plastic worms are eaten by as many as 25% of the bass that see them. Suggested range of inputs: 0.1 - 0.25

Step 6

Catchable Fish in Your Area: Step 6 estimates the number of fish that are going to be in the area that you are going to fish. Unless it is a small lake, most anglers only fish a small percentage of the total acreage that support bass. When we speak of acres of water being covered, we are not talking about how much water the boat covers, but how much water the lure covers. This number is determined by the time lures spend in the strike zone multiplied by the diameter of the strike zone. This variable is highly contingent upon the feeding mood of fish at a particular time. Inactive fish may have a strike zone as small as a few inches while active fish may chase down a lure from as far away as 50 feet. Since much of this information is unknowable until you are on the water, I've developed numbers through trial and error that I have found to be generally accurate. My best estimates are that with fast moving baits anglers can effectively cover as much as 8-14 acres of water per hour. With slower moving baits, such as Texas rigged soft plastics, particularly in cold water it could be as low as 4-8 acres of water per hour. Suggested range of inputs: 4-14 acres per hour

Step 7

Fisherman's Bonus: is a calculation that attempts to measure the skill of the angler. An angler that has fished a body of water their entire life certainly knows a lake far better than an individual who has only ever looked at a topographical map.

An input of 1 would be appropriate for an average angler who has never fished a lake. An input of 2 or more might be an estimate for a professional angler or someone who has fished the lake many times. Suggested range of inputs: 1-2

Step 8

The Pressure Factor: This step estimates the impact of fishing pressure on a body of water. As we have discussed at length previously, fishing pressure has one the biggest impacts of any variable as it relates to catch rates. Remember fishing pressure can be influenced in multiple fashions. You can choose to fish on low-pressure days, low-pressure lakes, or low-pressure areas or times of higher pressure lakes. The fishing pressure scale ranks from 1 to 3 with 1 being the lowest pressure water anglers typically encounter, on weekends these would likely be limited to private lakes or remote or difficult to get to bodies of water. 3s are extremely pressured lakes, they can occur on many popular lakes in the summer due to pleasure boaters or lakes hosting large fishing tournaments. An average lake on an average weekend near a metropolitan area is probably a 2. Those same lakes on a Wednesday may well be a 1. Very frequently lakes will have values somewhere between 1.5 and 2.0. If you plan to fish a pressured "3" lake on the weekend, but plan to fish offshore locations in the 8-13 foot range, it is possible the lake could drop down to a 1 or 2. This variable is inputted as a fraction over 1. Low pressure 1/1 = 1 high pressure = 1/3 = 0.2 or 20%. Suggested range of inputs: 1 - 0.2.

Step 9

Landing Percentage: This step is the last variable, and estimates the number of hooked fish that you are likely to land.

Typically baits with treble hooks have lower landing percentages than single hook baits. Landing percentages can vary widely by the gear and skill of the angler. In general, though, I have found treble hook landing percentages to range from 60-85%, and I've found single hook landing percentages to range from 75-90%. Suggested Range of Inputs: 0.6 - 0.9.

In the example provided on page 115 a fisherman fished a moderately pressured 1200 acre lake in the summer with a crankbait covering 8 acres per hour. The bass equation estimates the angler should land approximately 1.95 fish per hour. Working through this process takes time, and it is not an exercise I would recommend High Percentage Fishermen go through every time they head out to a lake. Thinking through the variables once per season is probably sufficient to provide anglers with baseline expected catch rates for a particular body of water. On new lakes, the tool can help you estimate catch rates before hitting the water, and might trigger a change in tactics if you find yourself underperforming. For lakes you fish on a regular basis the tool will drive home the point that the only variable that changes significantly from one outing to the next is fishing pressure. **Fishing low-pressure scenarios is the single greatest High Percentage tool you have in your arsenal.**

Closing Thoughts

"Bragging may not bring happiness, but no man having caught a large fish goes home through an alley."
-Ann Landers

In his book, "Tracking Trophies," John Hope said, "In the early years of the tracking program on Houston County Lake there were, at one time, nine fish over 7lbs with transmitters. All nine of these fish were caught over a two-year period by average fishermen. But it took two years to do it and all nine were caught during the two spawning seasons. Not a single fish was caught during any other time of the year. These fish did not leave the lake after the spawn. They didn't quit feeding for the rest of the year and they didn't hide in some deep, dark hole in the lake. They were in the lake year round. They weren't caught at any other time of the year simply because when bass reach trophy size they change their feeding habits, but by and large bass fishermen don't change theirs. "

I believe this quote perfectly sums up the chess board from the perspective of High Percentage Fishermen. Fishing is often viewed as a sport ruled by luck. The degree of success we achieve while fishing is not doomed to be controlled by the whims of the wind or the cycles of the moon. I believe as High Percentage Fishermen we have the ability to manufacture our own luck by leveraging the lessons of great anglers before us and by making data-based decisions on the water.

Throughout this book, I have argued that natural phenomena like weather and moon cycles have a comparatively small impact on fishing catch rates as compared to manmade factors such as fishing pressure. If I've failed to persuade you on this point, let me offer up one final piece of evidence. I examined years worth of Bassmasters Elite Series tournament results and compared catch rates over the course of the tournaments. On average, day 3 weigh-ins were 20% lower than day 1 weigh-ins. Are we to assume that the start of each tournament always had better weather or a more favorable moon phase than the end? Of course, this is not the case. The obvious variable at play here is fishing pressure. There is also a strong correlation (0.53) with the degree of the decline in catch rates as related to the size of the body of water. As you've probably guessed, smaller bodies of water show sharper declines in weigh-ins over the course of the tournament. Acres divided by boats. It's simple math. The facts are very clear on this matter. It's all about pressure folks. The best fishermen in the world catch fewer and smaller bass as fishing pressure increases regardless of the local weather conditions. This effect is magnified considerably for less skilled anglers. I believe High Percentage Fishing is the best method available to help combat ever-growing pressure on our finite bass resources.

All together I have spent the better part of three years collecting and analyzing data to write this book. I have learned an enormous amount about the sport and I've put more and bigger fish in the boat as a result. It is my sincere hope that something in this book will help you do the same.

I have tried my best, wherever possible to present my findings in a clear and concise manner. What I have written here, I believe to be true based on the best available information. The beautiful thing about science is that as new information becomes available our previous theories can be put to the test. New data will either reinforce our previous theories or we will be forced to modify or invent new ones. In any case, we will continue to learn and become better fishermen as a result. I have no doubt this process will play out into perpetuity as long as curious folks enjoy wetting a line.

R. alwine

10 Laws of High Percentage Fishing

1. Make data-based decisions
2. Minimize pressure
3. Avoid weather shocks
4. Avoid cold muddy water
5. Fish peak periods (morning/evening)
6. Fish the best bodies of water
7. Look for stability in weather
8. The wind is your friend (up to a point)
9. Live bait, trolling, & anchoring as trophy tactics
10. Don't forget about the night bite!

About The Author

Josh Alwine is a lifetime fisherman, who currently resides in Houston, Texas with his family. He has a degree in Industrial Engineering from Purdue University, a Master's Degree in Business from Marquette University, and has achieved a Black Belt certification in Lean Six Sigma. He currently works as a Director of Operations for a large industrial conglomerate overseeing manufacturing plants in several states. He's fished as far south as the Florida Keys and as far north as Canada chasing a variety of fresh and saltwater game fish.